Empowering TRIathletes To LEAD

Breaking The Cycle of Poverty In Urban Communities

Dr. Tekemia Dorsey

Empowering TRIathletes To LEAD

Copyright © 2021

Dr. Tekemia Dorsey, Halee Simons, &
Beloved Joshua Simons

FOREWORD

I first met Dr. Tekemia Dorsey through the work of my husband, Marlon who is a coach and board member for IABT. Because of my responsibilities as a wife, a mother of two young children, a full-time employee, and a graduate student, I have always stayed in the background of IABT. While Dr. Dorsey respected my position, she did not allow me to stay hidden. She saw my strengths, even from the sideline. Because of my high regard for her, I would sometimes wonder why she would call upon me for advice or to perform certain tasks, such as writing this foreword. I now understand that she sees somet0hing greater in me. Dr. Dorsey has a wonderful way of bringing forward the people who have accepted their place in the background and allowing them to rise to the occasion.

It has been a true honor to have crossed paths with Dr. Dorsey. She is one of the few pioneers who is diligent, relentless, and dedicated to the advancement of the next generation of future leaders. She is not only an honorable triathlete and coach, but also a magnificent teacher and educator. Dr. Dorsey has been called to do the work, which is still evolving in her, of introducing the sport of triathlon to urban youth and urban communities, all while raising academic achievement, leadership skills, and cultural awareness. As a graduate student studying Elementary Education, I recognize the importance of having a healthy cultural perspective when working with the youth of today. Regardless of a child's race, socioeconomic status, gender, abilities, disabilities, height, or weight, Dr. Dorsey will discover a place for him or her to flourish. I cannot think of anyone more worthy of advocating for our youth and the multisport industry. She is truly operating in her gift with strength and honor from above. Now prepare to be enlightened, motivated, and encouraged as you flow through the pages of this awe-inspiring book.

Marshall Denise Turner

"Before you are a leader, success is all about growing yourself. When you become a leader, success is all about growing others."

Jack Welsh

ABOUT THE AUTHOR

Dr. Tekemia Dorsey was elected in 2019 as the first African American to serve on the USA Triathlon Board of Directors. In 2006, Dorsey founded DTD's Urban Multisport Consulting Firm to provide full-service solutions to their ideal client and has a 501C3 nonprofit organization called, The International Association of Black Triathletes (IABT).

She is also the owner of IABT Multisport Racing, the only African American and woman-owned multisport racing company in the nation. Dr. Dorsey is a USA Triathlon Level 2 Endurance and Youth & Junior-certified coach, Youth & Junior Elite Coach, a USA Triathlon-certified Level 2 race director, USAT Board Liaison to the Age Group Nationals Committee, and a member of the USA Triathlon Race Director Committee. Dr. Dorsey is a graduate of Leadership Baltimore County, Class of 2020. Dorsey is the 2021 Recipient of the "No Quitters Club" Honors through the University of Phoenix.

Dr. Dorsey is a founding member of USA Triathlon's Diversity, Equity, Inclusion and Access Advisory Council, a 10-strong group of leaders across the multisport community who provide insight and perspective to shape USA Triathlon's DEIA initiatives. She is also the recipient of the 2020 USA Triathlon Women's Committee Diversity & Inclusion Award. Dr. Dorsey was nominated and selected as the 2020 Rings of Gold Award – Individual winner. The Rings of Gold Award – Individual recognized as an individual dedicated to helping children develop their Olympic or Paralympic dreams and reach their highest athletic and personal potential by the United States Olympic and Paralympic Committee.

Dr. Dorsey is the founder of the 2018 Youth & Junior TRI-Conference®/EXPO*Event. For 10 years she served on the Board of Directors for the Co-Ed Christian Softball League and for the remaining five years, she served as Commissioner of Co-Ed Christian Softball League overseeing 15 teams and 600+ players. In her role, she was also liaison to Baltimore City Recreations and Parks and Baltimore City Umpire League. Dr. Dorsey is the former CEO/Senior Consultant of The Creative GRP, LLC now DTD's Urban Multisport Consulting Firm. Under Dorsey's leadership, The Creative GRP, LLC is the seven-time recipient of the Best of Baltimore Small Business Consulting Award; the 2016 Recipient of the USCA Best of Baltimore Training Award; and was inducted into The Best of Baltimore Business Hall of Fame.

Dr. Dorsey received her Doctorate of Management in Organizational Leadership from the University of Phoenix and Masters of Education in Guidance & Counseling from the University of Maryland Eastern Shore. Using her leadership principles and core pillars, Dr. Dorsey has become an established, best-selling and awarding winner author and business professional, international keynote speaker, facilitator/workshop presenter, curriculum specialist, publisher, professor, entrepreneur, radio show host, executive leadership trainer/coach, community activist, athlete and Child of God. She is a well-rounded athlete as a runner (marathoner), duathlete, triathlete, and an IRONMAN. Dorsey has more than 28 years in working with youth, education, leadership, and sports.

DEDICATION

This book is dedicated to my children from which this journey started and continues with. Through them I have come to learn, to witness and to believe that youth of today is only as great as those that are willing to give them a chance of experiencing new adventures outside of the norm. Youth will rise to the occasion if adults simply allow them to do so. Thank you, Beloved Joshua, Halee, and Heaven Simons for being the leaders you are from the beginning, and it has been my pleasure and honor to be your mom, coach, and business mentor. The best is yet to come!

To my oldest son, Brandon J. from which this journey started with him more than 22 years ago from which a true foundation of understanding and framework for leadership, sports and youth begin and evolved. Thank you for teaching me to be my very best as a mom, Coach, Educator, and Leader.

This book is also dedicated to all the urban youth and urban communities that have yet to discover the sport of triathlon. The sport itself lends a credence far more extraordinary than any single disciplined sport and the discovery along the way is extraordinary. When give an opportunity to explore, I encourage you to embrace it full throttle so that no matter the outcome, you will understand firsthand the impact through the process of the untapped potential in SELF.

"While nothing is perfect or complete in the battle for civil rights, the efforts of Dr. King and those like him have in fact, changed the country and the world for the better in noticeable ways. His vision has made the world a more equal place, and if not equal, it has helped to ensure that minorities have a voice."

-Skai Jackson

BOOK DESCRIPTION

The 2nd book in this series, Empowering TRIathletes to Lead; Breaking the Cycle of Poverty In Urban Communities demonstrates how the triathlon sport used as a foundation in programming positively contributes to the transition of urban youth in behavior, leadership, advocacy and civil engagement. Building on the foundation set in Thought Leader: The Future of the Urban Triathlon Sport (Simons & Simons, 2020), Dorsey shares Case Studies of a 360 degree of transition urban youth undertake that helps them prepare for the real world. Using Dorsey's Leadership Models (2006) derived from a theoretical and conceptual framework, Dorsey's nine pillars walk urban youth through a metamorphosis process that yielded far greater results and transformation as expected. Another case study highlights, youth ages 9-15 years old from three of the largest urban cities in Maryland that engaged in a summer hybrid and fall program that transformed their community, their family, and most importantly, themselves.

Building on the phenomenological research completed in awarding of the author's doctoral degree (2006), the case study expands on the previous research while yielding greater results for the targeted population of underserved/underrepresented youth. The purpose of the program was to combat barriers preventing underrepresented/underserved youth from success through the triathlon sport. The program design included (1) Leadership Training & Development Through STEM, (2) Workforce Development Education & Certification, (3) Career and College Readiness, (4) Health and Wellness, and a (5) Community and Civic Engagement Project.

Data was collected via pre and posttest, parental feedback, participants' journal entries, unit exit tickets, feedback from partner organization, and more qualitative data such as interviews, collection of completed assignments, cognitive and behavioral changes documented from beginning to end. After 26 years in education (K-12 & Higher Education), 26 years working with youth in urban settings, 31 years in sports (athlete and coach), the author's hypothesis is that youth can rise to the occasion earlier in their formative years versus their latter success and have far greater success as they progress in life than what is previous documented in research.

The goal of 80% graduating from the program and demonstrating a change in mental, physical, intellect, and behavior. There were limitations due to its hybrid structure and buy-in from youth/parents. Based on the author's hypothesis, validity exists that provides a baseline to continue research with the current targeted population and research design with other youth across the United States.

Based on the author's hypothesis, validity exists that allows a deeper understanding that quality research was achieved and provides a baseline to continue research with the current targeted population and research design with other youth across the United States. This is recommended that this program is replicated to increase benefits to the targeted audience. Preparation programs for youth are highly needed due to the most recent statistics and the CoVid19 Pandemic has demonstrated that having degrees and lacking skill sets for adults were not enough to decrease high unemployment rates therefore, if we do not change the focus with our youth, those living in poverty will increase sufficiently in the years to come placing youth and families in more despite conditions than CoVid19.

Be sure to pick up the Empowering TRIathletes To Lead: Breaking the Cycle of Poverty in Urban Communities WORKBOOK! The workbook is designed for youth ages 10 plus as a preparation tool to plant the seeds in concepts key to life's success. Used with this book, the workbook is the right combination to assist urban youth in breaking the cycle of poverty while preparing their lives through changed behavior, mindset, advocacy, leadership, and civic engagement. Youth are able to create their own blueprint and framework for their future education, career, and societal endeavors.

There is also a TEACHER's EDITION for purchase to use to implement the curriculum successfully.

Be sure to pick up the 1st Book in the series – *Thought Leader: The Future of the Urban Triathlon Sport* and the 3rd Book/Workbook Series – *A Dive Deep: An Urban Multisport Impact. The Infrastructure That Changed The Trajectory & Narrative For Urban Youth, Urban Communities and Their Urban Futures.*

Order NOW www.urbanmultisportconsulting.com

Table of Contents

LEADERSHIP THROUGH LEGACY 2

WHAT IS CHILD DEVELOPMENT? 3

    Cognitive Development 4

    Social and Emotional Development 4

    Speech and Language Development.. 4

    Fine Motor Skill Development 4

    Gross Motor Skill Development 5

THE PROBLEM 6

    The Chosen Age Group 6

    Elementary School Culture 9

    Middle School Culture 9

    High School Culture 10

WHAT IS POVERTY? 12

WHAT IS AN URBAN COMMUNITY? 16

    1. Large size and high density of population: 16

    2. Heterogeneity: 16

    3. Anonymity: 16

    4. Mobility and transiency: 16

    5. Formality of relations: 17

    6. Social distance: 17

    7. Regimentation: 17

    8. Segmentation of personality: 17

    9. Family: 17

    10. Marriage: 18

    11. Occupation: 18

12.	Class extremes:	18
13.	Social heterogeneity:	18
14.	Social distance:	18
15.	System of interaction:	18
16.	Mobility:	19
17.	Materialism:	19
18.	Individualism:	19
19.	Rationality:	19
20.	Anonymity:	19
21.	Norm and social role conflict:	20
22.	Rapid social and cultural change:	20
23.	Voluntary associations:	20
24.	Formal social control:	20
25.	Secularization of outlook:	20
26.	Urban areas provide impulses for modernization in society as a whole.	20

WHAT IS THE TRIATHLON/MULTISPORT? 24
The History and Background of Triathlons 24

THE IMPACT OF SPORTS ON THE DEVELOPMENT OF CHILDREN 26
Physical Health 26
Children's Mental Health 26
Social Skills 27

The Chart of Progression through the Sport of Triathlon 28

Benefits of the Sport of Triathlon for Adults & Youth 32
Better physical health 32
Improved mental health 32

Weight loss	32
Less risk of injuries	33
Improved motivation to exercise	33
Develop multidisciplinary skills	33
Inspire others	33
Benefits of the Sport of Triathlon for Urban Youth	**34**
Youth Ages 3-6	35
Youth Ages 7-12	37
Junior 13-18	38
Collegiate 19-24	40
Age Group 25-29	40
Life Choice 30+	41
The Impact The Sport of Triathlon Could Have In Urban Communities	**42**
Disparity In Progression Between Cultures In the Sport of Triathlon	**43**
Prevention vs. Intervention and Postvention Efforts	47
CASE STUDIES	**50**
THE FUTURE OF THE URBAN TRIATHLON SPORT	50
LEADERSHIP	**53**
Personal Gratification from the Sport	**56**
THE BIRTHING OF THE	**58**
IABT JUNIOR MULTISPORT CLUB	**58**
THE CHANGE IS HERE	**60**
The PROBLEM	**61**
INCREASED OPPORTUNITIES	**63**
AN INTERVIEW WITH THE CO-FOUNDERS OF THE IABT JUNIOR MULTISPORT CLUB	**65**

INTRODUCTION	68
INSPIRATION	72
MOTIVATION	73
RACING WITH A NEUROLOGICAL TICK DISORDER	76
BEING AFRICAN AMERICAN & FEMALE	80
BEING AFRICAN AMERICAN & MALE	86
MAKING HISTORY IN THE SPORT	89
THE LOVE OF THE TRIATHLON SPORT	91
NCAA Women's Varsity Triathlon Programs	94
African American Fe/Males -TRI Collegiate Club	96
PASSING THE TORCH TO THE NEXT GENERATION	98
CASE STUDY #2 DR. TEKEMIA DORSEY'S SPORT ACADEMY 4 URBAN YOUTH	101
PROGRAM BENEFITS OF LEADERSHIP TRAINING AND DEVELOPMENT	104
PROGRAM BENEFITS OF WORKFORCE DEVELOPMENT PROGRAMS	106
PROGRAM BENEFITS OF	108
MENTORING FOR YOUTH	108
PROGRAM BENEFITS OF TUTORING	109
PROGRAM BENEFITS OF CAREER AND COLLEGE READINESS PROGRAMS	112
PROGRAM BENEFITS OF HEALTH AND WELLNESS PROGRAMS	113
CONCEPTUAL COMPONENT SUMMARIES	115
WHAT'S THE RELATIONSHIP BETWEEN DTD'S TRANSFORMATIONAL LEADERSHIP MODELS AND LEADERSHIP DEVELOPMENT?	118
Brief History - DTD's Transformational Leadership Models	120 |//

DR. TEKEMIA DORSEY'S (DTD) TRANSFORMATIONAL LEADERSHIP

MODELS 121

Definition of Terms 123

CORE PILLAR 1: WHO AM I? 125

The Struggle 126

a. Mental 127

b. Physical Struggle 127

b. Spiritual Struggle 128

Johari's Windows 129

CORE PILLAR 2: CRITICAL THINKING 131

Semi Aggressive Family Schedule 132

Aggressive Family Schedule 133

Howard Gardner's Multiple Intelligence Simple Grid 134

CORE PILLAR 3: TEAM BUILDING 135

Semi Aggressive Family Schedule 136

Aggressive Family Schedule 136

It Takes a Village 137

CORE PILLAR 4: CULTURAL DIVERSITY 139

CORE PILLAR 5: REAL WORLD EVENTS/SPIRITUAL GUIDANCE 142

Real World Events 142

Spiritual Guidance 144

CORE PILLAR 6: LEADERSHIP ATTRIBUTES 145

Great Leaders... 149

CORE PILLAR 7: COMMUNICATION 150

Sender - Receive Message 151

Communication Barriers 151

The Internet 152

CORE PILLAR 8: BEING TRANSFORMATIONAL 155
    Johari's Windows 157
CORE PILLAR 9: WHO AM I - 360 DEGREES OF EVOLUTION 158
    Become an Entrepreneur 158
DR. TEKEMIA DORSEY'S SPORTS ACADEMY 4 URBAN YOUTH 162
    Why are these components important? 162
    Employable Skills vs. Degrees During a Pandemic 162
        Summer Hybrid Program Expectations 163
    Initial Program Overview 164
        Adapted Version - Program Focus 164
        Initial Program Dates 164
        Adapted Program Dates 164
        Initial Program Design 164
    Program Design 165
    Foundational Principles 166
    Adapted Program Design 167
    Fall Program Experience 168
        Adapted Program Design 168
        Summation 169
        Organizational Impact 169
URBAN YOUTH PERSPECTIVE 172
    Special Needs Population 176
    Key transition skills 176
    Dr. Tekemia's Dorsey's (DTD) Sports Academy 4 Urban Youth 177
    Advocacy, Leadership, and Breaking The Cycle of Poverty Through The Triathlon Sport 178
        Education & Post-Secondary Plan Options 179

How do you get your child a 504 plan? 180
1. Document your child's needs. 180
2. Find out who the school's 504 coordinator is. 180
3. Write a formal request for a 504 plan. 180
4. Follow up on your request. 181
5. Go through the 504-plan evaluation process. 181
6. Meet with the school to see if your child qualifies. 181
7. Work together to create the 504 Plan. 181
Individual Education Plan (IEP) 181
Individual Transition Plan (ITP) 182
What types of assessments are used to develop the transition plan? 182
The four principal components of a Transition Planning Project Plan are: 183
Key Elements to the Transition Planning and the IEP 183
What is secondary transition and why is it important for students with disabilities? 183
Why Is Transition Planning Important in Special Education? 184
What Is Transition Planning? 184
Why is Transition Planning Important? 184
What are specific transition services examples? 185
What are transition skills? 185
What are the most important factors in determining the success of an individualized transition plan? 185
What is the difference between a postsecondary and an annual transition goal? 185
What types of organizations must be included in the transition plan to support the student's goals? 186
What IDEA says about transition planning? 186
What is transition planning in school? 186

What is transition planning and why is it important? 186

What is the purpose of the individual transition plan? 187

SPECIAL ED TRANSITION PLANNING: 188

FIVE KEYS TO SUCCESS 188

    A New Initiative 188

    Five Keys to Successful Transition Planning 189

        1: Student Involvement 189

        2: Self-advocacy 189

        3: Goal Setting 190

        4: Self-monitoring 190

        5: Self-determination 191

    Conclusion 191

Become A Corporate Executive 192

The Balancing Act for Moms 196

BECOME A LEADER IN YOUR COMMUNITY 198

BECOME A BETTER STUDENT 200

EXCEL IN THE WORKPLACE 202

FROM ORDINARY TO EXTRAORDINARY 205

"Preparation programs for youth are highly needed due to the most recent statistics and the CoVid19 Pandemic has demonstrated that having degrees and lacking skill sets for adults were not enough to decrease high unemployment rates therefore, if we do not change the focus with our youth, those living in poverty will increase sufficiently in the years to come placing youth and families in more despite conditions than CoVid19", says CEO,Dr.TekemiaDorsey

LEADERSHIP THROUGH LEGACY

Our maternal, paternal, and civil rights ancestors fought a good fight and paved the way for who we are today and who we are destined to become as we walk this earth. On the backs of their sweat, hard work, advocacy, sacrifices, and betrayal, doors have been opened, and glass ceilings continue to be broken. With each generation, the cycle continues for a better tomorrow.

The first level of modeling, coaching, and training as a person, being a part of a team, learning and mastering the art of communication, understanding diversity within a culture, learning to be independent yet dependent in a safe learning environment to think through the process to a result, etc. starts at home.

The second level of training and continuity is then transferred to the school setting. Being a part of a team, enhancing communication, understanding the diversity within cultures, and learning to think critically on a grander scale begins. It can be frightening and overwhelming, but one navigates as best one can.

The third level of training requires integration of home and school with real-world experiences and whether one is prepared or not. Although real-world experiences occur at home and in school, as one grows wiser with age, a greater expectation of knowing and acting comes into play. The third level of training is the stage of life where things seem to take a turn, either for the best or worst.

Training happens daily and is expected to be better with the generations; however, there is a gap between the second and the third levels that widen versus closes the inequalities and disparities of life, especially for youth and those living in urban communities.

The single variable often witnessed in life working with youth remains the age of introduction. Most programs designed for preparation are introduced much later in life, directly impacting the outcome. Some believe the age of cognitive development hinders the understanding and aptitude of the content to age groups. On the contrary, theory infused with practical application is how learning occurs best from the dawn of time. It starts from the home, with transferable traits to the school setting and finally in life, so what makes a more refined approach in terms of a preparation program any different? No such disparity should not exist, but it does.

"Minorities have a right to appeal to the Constitution as a shield against such oppression."

-James K. Polk

WHAT IS CHILD DEVELOPMENT?

Child development is a process every child goes through that involves learning and mastering skills like sitting, walking, talking, skipping, and tying shoes. Children learn these skills, called developmental milestones, during predictable periods.

As children progress during their developmental milestones, they can rise to the expected levels of life with at least an adequate understanding of self. The development milestones do not stop after the children develop into the latter years of life; it continues during one's development span of life.

Children develop skills in five main areas of development:

Cognitive Development

Cognitive development is the child's ability to learn and solve problems. For example, this includes a two-month-old baby learning to explore the environment with hands or eyes or a five-year-old learning how to do simple math problems.

Social and Emotional Development

Social and emotional development is the child's ability to interact with others, including helping themselves and self-control. Examples of this type of development would include: a six-week-old baby smiling, a ten-month-old baby waving bye-bye, or a five-year-old boy knowing how to take turns in games at school.

Speech and Language Development

Speech and language development is the child's ability to understand and use language. For example, this includes a 12-month-old baby saying his first words, a two-year-old naming parts of her body, or five-year-old learning to say "feet" instead of "foots."

Fine Motor Skill Development

Fine motor skill development is the child's ability to use small muscles; specifically, their hands and fingers, pick up small objects, hold a spoon, turn pages in a book, or use a crayon to draw.

Gross Motor Skill Development

Gross motor skill development is the child's ability to use large muscles. For example, a six-month-old baby learns how to sit up with some support, a 12-month-old baby learns to pull up to a stand holding onto furniture, and a five-year-old learns to skip.

The National Center on Birth Defects and Developmental Disabilities has recently launched a campaign to promote child development.

The developmental milestones take a 360-degree transformation for children in the early stages of life and adults in their latter stages. The five developmental milestones serve as a foundation of understanding that remains constant in life over time. When infused with knowledge, one has the opportunity to grow personally and professionally to new heights.

THE PROBLEM

There is a lack of comprehensive, quality enriched preparation programs founded on a theoretical/conceptual framework to address the gaps needed for urban youth to succeed in life and avoid entering and overcoming the cycle of poverty.

Youth and parents are unaware of the knowledge that correlates to real-world experience and academic expectations with short-term and long-term success. Youth and parents are unaware of the missed opportunities awaiting them. Youth are unaware of the bleak future before it is too late.

Youth tend to receive the education and access to information later than needed. When the information is received, its overwhelming, and youth cannot understand its applicability to the real world. Information sharing with youth that allows them not just theory but practical application in a safe environment before entering the world of work would increase their success as adults. Unfortunately, what should, could, or would is not as easily accessible as one would like and for various reasons. These reasons include lack of resources, lack of personnel, lack of funding, lack of partnerships, lack of knowledge, lack of understanding, lack of training opportunities, and the list continues.

There are preparation programs that touch on many topics that complement the growth and development of youth across the US. There are topics within preparation programs that are explored year-round, but there is a lack of opportunities for consistent programming and execution made available to youth ages 10-15 years old.

The Chosen Age Group

Poverty, education, and sports impact people from all walks of life. Each variable individually and collectively can and has had long-term impacts. As we think of targeted populations that will grow to live below the poverty line before age 18 possibly, we move from generalization to specific age groups to plant the seed for success and break poverty.

The elementary school age is too young, and the latter years of high school are too old, but the middle school and early years of high school remain key to long-term success if captured. Many adults will say that the middle school-aged years are too young because mentally, emotionally, physically, socially, and academically students on this level are not ready. The same can be said for high school-age youth but argued differently for middle school-age youth. The gap that lends to the argument of middle versus high school and the appropriate age groups remains the foundation and exposure of the youth from their families. Honestly, every student is made of different clothes and should not be placed in a category other than who they are and what they bring to the table.

On May 5, 1997, Dr. Dorsey submitted her master's thesis entitled "The Roles and Functions That School Counselors Play in Preventing and Remediating Stressors Among Middle School Students" in partial fulfillment of the requirements for the Master of Education Degree in Guidance and Counseling, Education Department at the University of Maryland Eastern Shore.

In the master's thesis introduction, Dorsey wrote, "Children today live in a hectic and changing world, quite different from what it was a few decades ago. They are growing up much faster and must live up to the expectations and demands of teachers, parents, peers, and society. Children are often forced to adjust to numerous adverse situations without much assistance, such as communication barriers, peer pressure, and school-related problems. These situations can be highly confusing and frustrating. Many circumstances, including wanting to be accepted by friends, not doing well academically, not being allowed to think and make decisions, parents not understanding them, and not having enough autonomy, increase the children's anxieties (Bauewens and Hourcade, 1992; Elkind, 1986; Omizo, Omizo, and Suzuki, 1988; Lupton-Smith, Carruthers, Goettee, and Modest, 1996; and Kiselica, Baker Thomas and Reedy, 1994).

Culturally diverse children represent a significant part of the school population at risk of mental illness due to stress-related factors. Generally, these families tend to have limited support services, and they tend not to use the support services available (Kopala, Esquivel, and Baptiste, 1994). School counselors need to be prepared to cope with this societal change. Schools will not be able to hire enough culturally diverse counselors for the school populations; therefore, school counselors will increasingly have to counsel students from cultures different from their own. Counselors with the amount of cultural diversity expected, learning about the many different cultures will be a difficult task. On the other hand, helping culturally diverse students to overcome barriers to education and maximize their probability of success is beneficial (Cochran, 1996).

To assist children with stress and stressful situations in their lives, school counselors, in a collaborative team effort with teachers, parents, administrators, and students, accurately determine what the stress is and identify strategies to reduce stress. School counselors assist students in coping with stress as well. Research suggests that learning how to cope successfully is a vital determiner of the long-term psychological, emotional, and physiological effects of stress (Henderson, Kelbey, and Engrebretson, 1992)" (pp. 1-2).

Dorsey's research focused on middle school students as the targeted population, and at that time, her passion for students on this level was not as strong as it had grown over the years. After completing her master's in education, Dorsey went on to work on the high school level, elementary school level, a high school within the middle school level, and on higher education levels (master's and doctoral level).

Dorsey's 2006 dissertation entitled "The Academic Achievement Differences of Racial/Ethnic and Gender of 5th Grade Students; A Phenomenological Case Study" focused on education during her doctoral degree.

Dorsey chose the fifth grade as the focal point of her dissertation studies to extend the research explored during her master's degree and, at this juncture in her career, had extended her knowledge-based and experience as a certified school counselor in an urban setting an entire decade before completing her doctoral studies. Dorsey had grown as an expert in the field, and the research acquired through her dissertation research and process enlightened and challenged her understanding on new levels.

Dorsey's dissertation and research unveiled the gaps in education and leadership she did not know. Interviewing leaders, educators, and teachers from public and non-public sectors within education; from varying districts within the same state and other states assisted in understanding concerns in education. The problems shared by educators and leaders identified what truly needed to be accomplished, and it also frustrated Dorsey because no approach other than dismantling education and starting over would ever suffice actual change. In 1982 during President Reagan's administration, he wanted to dismantle the State Department, aka the Department of Education, to implement the change needed for success effectively.

President Reagan wanted to dismantle the education department in the early 80s, and Dorsey was quite offended to read this information during her dissertation research. It was not the education department that needed to be dismantled; it was the education system in its entirety so that change could be equitable, and no child would indeed be left behind. Is it genuinely possible for no child to be left behind with a diverse culture as each state and sub-district has? No way. Children will always be left behind because the world, the education system, socioeconomic statuses of families, etc., are not equitable. However, there remains a way to break the cycle of doom for future generations, which may change the trajectory of groups of persons across the US.

Elementary School Culture

There are specific accolades for students when they reach fifth grade. They are viewed as the "cream of the crop, the upper echelon, and the school's leaders" simply because they have earned the rights and are viewed as the role models for the younger students. They have clawed their way through their early education years and are now prepared for the next journey in their progression. Notice that the variables did not mention their academic endeavors, athletic endeavors, physical appearance, psychological state of mind, or self-belief. These variables are not crucial to the student because they are ready to move on at this point in their lives. They no longer consider themselves children, and they remain unaware of what the next chapter presents or requires.

Middle School Culture

Although students exiting fifth grade are at the top of their game, their worlds are turned upside down when they enter sixth grade. No longer are they hand-held in their journey by the teachers, and no longer is the umbilical cord connected. The middle school culture is a complete shock to students, and they go from the top to the bottom overnight. In their case of going from the top to the bottom overnight, this happens during the summer months. Even more shocking is that they are separated from the security blankets that once gave them comfort, their friends, classmates, friends, acquaintances, familiarity with school culture, and the list continues because the next progression for students would be sixth grade. In most settings, sixth grade is the start of middle school. As students transition from fifth grade to sixth grade, many variables change.

Middle school-age youth enter a phase that is transformational and influential. Middle school is also a challenging period where youth are lost, uncertain, exploratory, afraid, vulnerable, frustrated, cautious, and impressionable. It is also the perfect time to plant the seed of short-term and long-term opportunities to connect the dots of academic, sports, employment, college and career, leadership, and community endeavors.

High School Culture

Culture in high school is one step closer to the real world, freedom, opportunity, and the unknown. When middle school students exit middle school to high school, it's an even more significant leap with more risks. Middle school-age youth have grown during their tenure from sixth to eighth grade and find themselves as the leaders, the upper echelon, cream of the crop, and role models to the younger students. However, as they prepare for the last step on their educational ladder before entering the real world, they are unaware of what truly awaits them on the other side. The difference is they have learned to navigate their independence and interdependence a little better, for the most part, from middle to high school versus elementary to middle school—the vast difference between middle school and high school with academics what is known as credits. Credits are earned and applied towards completing a high school diploma.

While students cannot wait until they exit high school, there are many hurdles and obstacles to be overcome to get there (graduation). Students entered the high school from their middle school days in one of several categories. These categories for students are seen as early as elementary, identified and tracked in middle school, and tracked further in high school. These categories can include AP/Honors, Standard, Special Needs/IEP, or a combination.

The chosen age group that fits best preparatory programs are youth ages 10 – 15 (9 and 16 depending on where their birth date falls). This age group is not too young nor too old but just in the right stage of their lives to plant the seed and grow the plant. Some may disagree with the chosen age group due to the lack of experience, age, maturity level, depth of understanding, cognitive functioning, and the list continues. On the contrary, others, such as the author, who have worked with youth for the past 20-plus years, can argue that this age group is ideal through Case Studies and data.

For the sake of this book, preparatory programs are defined as programs that focus on transition for youth.

What is missing along the way from elementary to middle school but touched on the service yearly in high school is the information needed close the gaps of life. The information needed for students to excel successfully in life and post-high school is not introduced to them early enough to have an impact and is often unavailable in time to students to avoid falling below and living in poverty. Once a person enters the poverty threshold, it becomes an ever-ending hamster wheel cycle of negativity. If a change does not occur sooner than later, generations fall within that same cycle of poverty.

WHAT IS POVERTY?

According to the 2019 Datausa Profile, 9.1% of Baltimore County residents live BELOW the Poverty Level; that is 73.6K of 808K Residents. Females ages 25-34 are leading the charge in living below the poverty level, closely followed by Females ages 18-24 and then Males ages 18-24. These numbers are detrimental to the current targeted population because of the lack of opportunities, limited barriers that existed before CoVid19, and heightened due to the CoVid19 Pandemic.

According to the 2018 US Census, under the category Poverty by Age, of the 175,286 Children in Baltimore County, 20,329 live in poverty (Poverty USA, 2020). According to the statistics, Baltimore County has experienced a 0.485% decline in population. These disparities are mainly due to the lack of equitable access to resources within and compared to other counties.

According to 2019 DataUSA, a comparison throughout the state of Maryland by Race & Ethnicity identifies the highest average salaries belong to (1) Asian (Average Salary - $73,898), (2) White (average Salary - $72,025), and (3) Native Hawaiian & Other Pacific Islanders (Average Salary - $67,828). Baltimore County's top three ethnic groups are white, black, and Hispanic in that order, but either of the latter two did not even make the Maryland listing. These statistics remain alarming at best. Blacks and Hispanics are primarily defined as under-served and under-represented populations.

According to The Governor's Office of Children's website (2020), Maryland's youth unemployment rate is more than three times its adult unemployment rate (4.9%). The number of 16- to 24-year-olds who are unemployed jumped following the recession. According to the FRED Economic Data (2019), although Baltimore County saw a considerable decline in youth unemployment from 2010 – to 2017, from 2018 – to 2019, there was a sharp increase in youth employment rates from more than 3%.

There are many reasons why young people are failing to enter Maryland's adult workforce, including but not limited to,
1. Skills mismatch between the skills that employers want and the skills that youth have,
2. Stiff competition with more experienced adults for entry-level or unskilled jobs, and
3. Individual barriers such as lack of a high school diploma or GED, caring for young children, transitioning from systems, lack of

transportation, or substance use, to name just a few.

Poverty in districts varies from city to city, county to county, district to district, country to country, and state to state. However, what remains constant is that poverty is absolute, and there are three categories of individuals susceptible to living below the poverty level.

The three categories of individuals that are at the top of living below the poverty line are:

1. Females: 24 – 35
2. Females: 18 – 24
3. Males: 18 – 24

When we think of poverty, there is an automatic connection with blacks, Hispanics, Asians, and other non-whites. Poverty is not a glue to minority honey. Poverty is natural for a particular culture of persons based on the environment in which they live. Poverty is not a stigma or should not be associated with the color of one's skin. Still, more so, the lack thereof affiliated with one's life, such as a lack of resources, a lack of funding flow, a lack of opportunities, to name a few. Poverty is more closely associated with urban communities than with white, black, Hispanic, Asian, or other races/cultures.

Before the Covid19 Pandemic, youth in urban communities worldwide faced disparities in overlapping areas to get ahead. Since the Covid19 Pandemic's arrival and continuance, the disparity gaps have widened for everyone but even more for those living in urban communities. Organizations have been forced to pivot programming to online or hybrid or close their doors. Some have survived, others have thrived, while a few continue to learn how to pivot to the digital age and others no longer are part of the conversation. The cycle of poverty has increased versus decreased for males and females within 18 – 34. The Covid19 Pandemic has shown that having a degree is not enough. Everyone, including those with Ph.D.'s, need to enhance their skillsets to survive.

If change is going to take place to improve our future, waiting for males and females to enter the range or while living below the poverty level is too late. Waiting for males and females to hit their later high school years is also too late. To make a difference in the world, we need more preparation programs for success instead of an intervention or postvention. Preparatory programs will indeed plant more seeds to break the cycle of poverty in many communities, especially urban ones. To understand the struggles and barriers of those living within urban communities, it remains essential to explore the characteristics comprised of urban areas.

Adversity. "Remember that not getting what you want is sometimes a wonderful stroke of luck."

—Dalai Lama.

WHAT IS AN URBAN COMMUNITY?

There are many ways to define an urban community; however, "An urban community can be defined as an area comprised of larger places and densely settled areas around them. Urban areas do not necessarily follow municipal boundaries".

Characteristics of urban communities with explanation are, but are not limited are:

1. Large size and high density of population:

The size of the urban community is much larger than the rural community. Not only this, in urban areas, there is a high density of population. Density increases the number of short-term, impersonal, and utilitarian social relationships a person is likely to have. Urbanity and density are positively correlated.

2. Heterogeneity:

The urban population is heterogeneous. It consists of various shades of people—different castes, classes, ethnic groups, religions, etc. They are not all alike. The urban community is noteworthy for its diversity.

3. Anonymity:

The sheer pressure of number marks for anonymity. Anonymity is a loss of identity and a sense of belongingness. The heterogeneity of city life with its mixture of people of all races, castes, classes, creeds, occupations, and ethnic origins heightens the sense of anonymity.

4. Mobility and transiency:

Urban life is dynamic. Social relations are temporary. Therefore, permanency does not develop in urban relations. There is a high rate of geographical and social mobility in urban areas. In America, on average, a person changes his job (occupational mobility) within six years.
Consequently, his dwelling (changes of residence) also changes. Different types of mobility usually mean transiency of contact. As such, urban social relations continue for a short time. Urban dweller continually makes new social contacts.

5. Formality of relations:

In urban social life, relations are not intimate, and kinship based. Most routine social contacts in the city are impersonal and segmented. Formal politeness takes the place of genuine friendliness. The impersonality of urban life is a necessary and convenient way of urban living.

6. Social distance:

City people are physically crowded but socially distant. Social distance is a product of anonymity, impersonality, and heterogeneity. Occupational differences maybe even more important sources of social distance. Urbanites become nigh dwellers, not neighbors. Apartment dwellers may live for years without any acquaintance with many other occupants.

7. Regimentation:

The city is always in a hurry. The urban community's life (work and entertainment) becomes 'clock regulated.' Order, regularity, and punctuality are the characteristics of urban life. His movement is controlled by traffic lights, railway stations, and other places by elevators and escalators on the streets.

8. Segmentation of personality:

Most routine urban contacts are of a secondary group rather than primary group nature. Most contacts are instrumental; we use another person as a necessary functionary to fulfill our purposes. We do not necessarily interact with entire persons but with people in terms of their formal roles as a postman, bus drivers, office assistants, police officers, and other functionaries. We thus interact with only a segment of the person, not with the whole person.

9. Family:

As far as the urban community is concerned, greater importance is attached to the individual than family. Nuclear families are more prevalent in urban areas.

10. Marriage:

In the case of urban communities, there is a preponderance of love marriages and inter-caste marriages. One also comes across a more significant number of divorces. Sons and daughters enjoy considerable freedom in choosing their life partners.

11. Occupation:

In the urban areas, the significant occupations are industrial, administrative, and professional. Divisions of labor and occupational specialization are standard in towns/cities/metropolises.

12. Class extremes:

In the words of Bogardus, "Class extremes characterize the city." A town and a city house the richest and the poorest of people. In a city, the slums of the poor exist alongside the rich's palatial bungalows amidst the middle-class members' apartments. The most civilized modes of behavior and the worst racketeering are found in the cities.

13. Social heterogeneity:

If villages symbolize cultural homogeneity, the cities symbolize cultural heterogeneity. The cities are characterized by diverse peoples, races, and cultures. There is excellent variety concerning the food habits, dress habits, living conditions, religious beliefs, cultural outlook, customs, and traditions of the urbanites.

14. Social distance:

Social distance is the result of anonymity and heterogeneity. Most of one's routine social contacts in a town or city are impersonal and segmentary. In the urban community, social responses are incomplete and half-hearted. There is an utter lack of personal involvement in the affairs of others.

15. System of interaction:

George Simmel held that the social structure of urban communities is based on interest groups. The circles of social contact are more comprehensive in the city than in the country. There is a broader area of interaction system per man and aggregate. This makes city life more complex and varied. City life is characterized by the predominance of secondary contacts and impersonal, casual, and short-lived relations. At any rate, the man in the street virtually loses his identity, being treated like a "number" having a specific "address."

16. Mobility:

The most important feature of an urban community is its social mobility. In urban areas, an individual's social status is determined not by heredity or birth but by merit, intelligence, and perseverance. Urbanity and mobility are positively correlated.

17. Materialism:

In the urban community, man's social existence revolves around wealth and material possessions. The worth of an urbanite today is being judged not by what he is but by what he has. Status symbols in financial assets, salaries, and costly home appliances count greatly for the urbanites.

18. Individualism:

The urbanites attach supreme importance to their welfare and happiness. They hesitate to think or act for the good of others.

19. Rationality:

In an urban community, there is an emphasis on rationality. People are inclined to reason and argue. Their relationship with others is governed, for the most part, by the consideration of gain or loss. A relationship takes place on a contractual basis. Once the contract is over, the human relationship automatically closes.

20. Anonymity:

As Bogardus observes, the "Urban groups have a reputation for namelessness." The urban community cannot be a primary group by size and population. Here nobody knows anybody, and nobody cares for anybody. The urbanites do not care for their neighbors and have nothing to do with their miseries or pleasures.

21. Norm and social role conflict:

The urban community is characterized by norm and social role conflict. Factors such as the size, density, and heterogeneity of the population, extreme occupational specialization, and the class structure prevalent in the urban context led to such a state of affairs.

Individuals or groups often seek divergent ends in the absence of uniform and fixed social norms. This has a considerable share in causing social disorganization.

22. Rapid social and cultural change:

Rapid social and cultural change characterize urban life. The importance attached to traditional or sacred elements has been relegated to the background. The benefits of urban life have affected changes in norms, ideologies, and behavior patterns.

23. Voluntary associations:

The urban community is characterized by impersonal, mechanical, and formal social contacts occurring among the people. Naturally, they have a strong desire to develop genuine social relationships to satisfy their hunger for emotional warmth and a sense of security. They form associations, clubs, societies, and other secondary groups.

24. Formal social control:

Social control in an urban community is essentially formal. Such agencies regulate individuals' behavior as police, jails, law courts, etc.

25. Secularization of outlook:

In cities, ritual and kinship obligations are diluted. Caste and community considerations yield to economic logic. This results in the secularization of outlook.

26. Urban areas provide impulses for modernization in society as a whole.

It understands the characteristics of urban communities, and the definition assists in setting the precedents and barriers faced by urban youth and families. There is also good to understand the rural-urban differences: demographic and socio-cultural characteristics!

Rural and urban communities are different based on several criteria like occupation, size, the density of population, environment, homogeneity-heterogeneity, social stratification, mobility, and system of interaction:
The term 'community' is used by sociologists to describe a quality of relationship which produces a strong sense of shared identity among persons living in a fixed geographical area. They describe 'rural' as a community and 'urban' as a society. When sociologists hold that society moves from traditional to modern, they contrast pre-industrial, largely rural, traditional society with industrial, predominantly urban, modern society.

While American sociologist Louis Wirth used the terms' rural and urban' for contrasting communities, German sociologist Ferdinand Toennies used' gemeinschaft and Gesellschafts,' M. Durkheim mechanical and organic' solidarity, and Talcott Parsons' traditional and modern' societies.

Wirth (1938), distinguishing urban from rural society, defined the term city in three fundamental features. These features are population size, density, and heterogeneity. These characteristics meant that though the city-dweller would experience more human contacts than the rural inhabitant, he would also feel more isolated because of their (contacts)' emotionally empty' nature.

According to Wirth, typical of the city, social interactions are impersonal, segmental (narrow in scope), superficial, transitory, and usually of a purely practical or 'instrumental' kind. He describes these as 'secondary' contacts, totally different from 'primary' contacts in rural areas. According to Max Weber, the most fundamental feature of a city functions as a marketplace and displays a relative predominance of trading-commercial relations.

Rural and urban communities are different based on several criteria like occupation, size, the density of population, environment, homogeneity-heterogeneity, social stratification, mobility, and system of interaction:

> (1) The main occupation of people in a rural community is agriculture, though a few people are also engaged in non-agricultural pursuits. People in urban communities are mainly engaged in non-agricultural pursuits like manufacturing, trade and commerce, service, and professions.
>
> (2) Rural communities are small, while urban communities are

larger. According to the 1991 census figures, in India, of the 74.27 percent population living in villages, 36.57 percent of villages have a population of less than 2,000, 21.37 percent between 2,000 and 5,000, and 13.33 percent more than 5,000. On the other hand, of the 25.73 percent population in urban areas, 0.72 percent of urban areas have less than 10,000 population, 5.27 percent between 10,000 and 50,000, 2.75 percent between 50,000 and one lakh, and 16.4 percent above 1 lakh (These figures exclude population of Assam and Jammu and Kashmir). The adverse size of a household in rural areas in 1991 was 4.9, and in urban areas, it was 4.4 members.

(3) Density of the population in a rural community is low (200 to 1,000 persons per square mile), while in the urban community, it is high (more than 1,000 persons per square mile).

(4) People in rural areas are close to nature, while people in urban areas are surrounded more by an artificial environment and are isolated from nature.

(5) Rural communities are more homogeneous while urban communities are more heterogeneous.

(6) While rural communities are stratified more on caste and less on a class basis, urban communities are stratified more on a class basis.

(7) Mobility in rural areas is more from villages to villages and cities, while mobility in urban areas is more from one city to another. In 1991, of the 225 million migrants in the country, 17.7 percent had migrated from rural to urban areas, 11.8 percent from urban-to-urban areas, 64.5 percent from rural-to-rural areas, and 6 percent from urban to rural areas.

(8) Relations amongst people in rural areas are predominantly personal and relatively durable, while in urban areas, relations are more secondary, impersonal, casual, and short-lived.

(9) The infant mortality rate in rural areas is one and a half times more than that in urban areas (80:49).

(10) Labor force participation rate in rural areas is more than three times that in urban areas. In 1993-94, it was 294 million in rural areas against 85.7 million in urban areas. It is a little less than three

times (189.3:67.3 million ratios). While among females, it is more than five times (104.7:18.4 million) Manpower Profile, India, 1998:129).

(11) The number of working children in the rural areas is ten times more than in the urban areas (In 1991, it was 10.26 to 1.03 million).

If we follow Toennies' terms gemeinschaft and Gesellschaft (1887), it may say that gemeinschaft relationships are typical of rural life and gesellschaft relationships of urban life. Characterized by the predominance of intimate primary relationships and emphasis on tradition, consensus, and informality describes bests a gemeinschaft-type rural community.

Social bonds are based on close personal ties of kinship and friendship. On the other hand, in the gesellschaft- type urban society, social relationships are formal, contractual, reasonable, and specialized. Urban society has a weak family organization and stresses practical goals and the impersonal and competitive nature of social relationships.

Durkheim's (1933) concepts of mechanical and organic solidarity denoted it may be said that solidarity in a rural community is mechanical and in an urban community is organic. The rural community based on mechanical solidarity is characterized by the homogeneity of values and behavior (i.e., everybody sharing the same religiously inspired beliefs and habits), solid social constraint, and loyalty to tradition and kinship. It is further characterized by simple division of labor, very little specialization of functions, only a few social roles, and little tolerance of individuality.

Based on organic solidarity, the urban community is characterized by a unity based on the interdependence of a considerable number of highly specialized roles and complex division of labor that requires the co-operation of almost all groups and individuals of the society.

Poverty is synonymous with urban communities and vice versa; however, this is not always the case. There are bright sides and success stories that come out of urban communities, even amid the Covid19 Pandemic.

One area contributing to the bright sides and success stories evolved from urban communities, especially in the Covid19 Pandemic, under Dr. Dorsey's leadership, includes the triathlon sport as a critical element for programming.

WHAT IS THE TRIATHLON/MULTISPORT?

Triathlon was invented in the early 1970s by the San Diego Track Club as an alternative workout to the rigors of track training. The club's first event consisted of a 10km run, an 8km cycle, and a 500m swim. Over the next decade, the triathlon's popularity continued to build, and it soon gained worldwide recognition.

The History and Background of Triathlons

A "triathlon" is defined as a three-part sports discipline comprising swimming, cycling, and running. The three sports are contested as a continuous event without a rest. The triathlon can be an individual or team event over varying distances. Triathlon history dates to the early 1970s and originated with the San Diego Track Club.

The triathlon was designed to be an alternative to hard track training. The first triathlon event was held on September 25, 1974. Don Shanahan and Jack Johnstone are pioneers in the history of the triathlon. The San Diego Track Club sponsored the event. The triathlon then comprised a 10 km run, 8 km cycle, and 500 m swim.

In 1989, the sport was awarded Olympic status and featured at the 2000 Sydney Olympics in Australia for the first time. Since then, the sport has grown in popularity. No other sport achieved Olympic status in such a short time. Over the next decade, the triathlon grew by leaps and bounds and soon gained recognition worldwide.

In 1989, the International Triathlon Union (ITU) was founded in Avignon, France, and the first official world championships were held. The official distance for the triathlon was set at a 1500 m swim, a 40 km cycle, and a 10 km run—taken from existing events in each discipline already on the Olympic program. This standard distance is used for the ITU World Cup series and featured at the Sydney Olympic Games.

Triathlon races are held over four distances: sprint, Olympic, long course, and ultra. The Olympic triathlon comprises a 1.5 km swim, a 40 km bike ride, and a 10 km run.

The race remains continuous after a mass start, with no stops between the three legs. Changeovers or transitions are vital to race strategy.

Women are expected to finish in just over 2 hours, with men requiring about 1 hour 50 minutes. The women race on the opening morning of the games, followed by the men the following day.

The triathlon sport is an event that encompasses two to three disciplines such as swim, cycle, and runs; run, cycle and run; swim and run; swim and bike (aquathon). In Dr. Dorsey's eyes, the beauty of this triathlon sport is that it speaks a universal language for all, especially youth in urban communities.

Unlike single disciplined sports, the triathlon sport caters to all. The sport has events for all types of people, regardless of social and economic disparities, skin color, religious affiliation, geographic location, or disability, and the list continues.

One of the concerns remains the triathlon sport is not widely known in urban communities or underserved and underrepresented communities. Another concern is how the triathlon sport can be used as a tool for success for urban youth due to its untapped potential as a sport and equally matched when used in a program.

THE IMPACT OF SPORTS ON THE DEVELOPMENT OF CHILDREN

Adults understand the necessity of staying physically active as we age. It not only keeps our bodies healthy and functioning optimally, but recent studies have found that physical activity can help prevent cognitive decline later in life.

Similarly, physical activity has an immense impact on not only children's physical health and development but also on their psychological health. Sport, more specifically, can have an even more significant impact in these areas of growth while improving social skills in the process.

Sport provides children with the perfect outlet to keep them active while having fun and learning valuable life skills. Below are how sports can help children grow physically, mentally, and socially.

Physical Health

To help physical aid development in early childhood, children need a balanced diet, plenty of sleep, and one hour of exercise each day. The physical benefits of doing so can have the following impact on children:

- Stronger muscles, bones & joints
- Stronger heart
- Controlled body fat
- Decreased risk of type 2 diabetes
- Improved fitness

Children's Mental Health

Along with the plethora of physical benefits, the mental benefits are equally impressive; when we are physically active, our body releases serotonin which directly contributes to our well-being.

Exercise has also been found to relieve stress, depression, and anxiety. Although often overlooked, children experience these emotions just as adults do, and exercise is a great way to help combat these feelings.

Sport increases the likelihood of children staying active, allowing them to sleep better and be mentally sharp. Recent studies have found that increased physical activity levels directly relate to school performance, particularly in math, reading, and retention of information.

Social Skills

Sport can help encourage children to be more physically active but also helps teach them valuable skills and life lessons that they can carry with them through to adulthood. Growing up can be difficult, leaving much youth with inadequacy, but the sport has been found to help increase self-esteem and self-confidence in children.

Not only does sport increase their confidence, but it also helps keep children social. Social skills that are learned or enhanced through sport while assisting children in growing into successful adults include:

- Teamwork
- Fair play
- Communication
- Respect for others
- Ability to follow rules
- Independence
- Leadership

Sports are a great way to keep children active, but they offer a few benefits that stretch much beyond that. Sport not only aids children in their development process but gives them the necessary skills to be successful later in life. If sports for urban youth to advance in life were enough, the content of this book and the experiences along the way would be useless.

THE CHART OF PROGRESSION THROUGH THE SPORT OF TRIATHLON

(USAT, ITU, Olympics)

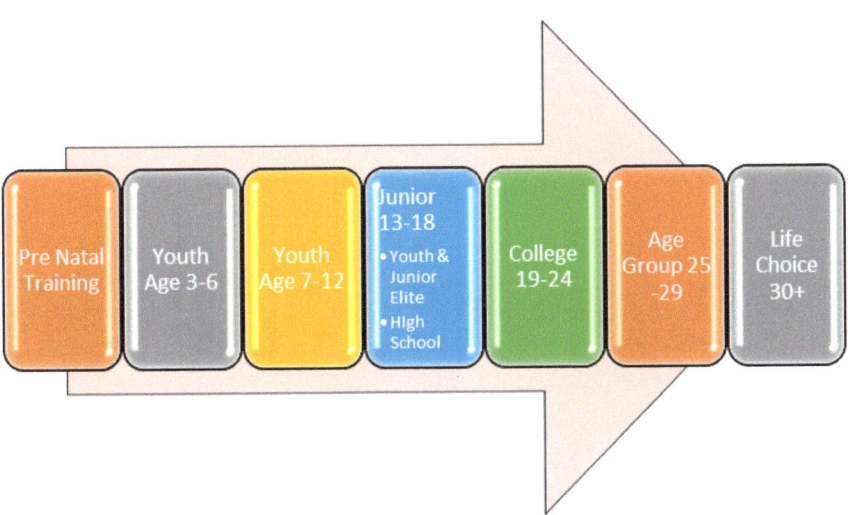

The author added Pre-Natal Training to this image because non-minority parents are already engaged in "ACTIVE" sports, general activity in life, and more equitable resources for youth in suburban and rural communities. What contributes to the increase of non-minorities in the sport of triathlon is the activity of parents and the introduction of the sport through the family tree versus the encouragement of the sport itself. Adult triathletes impregnated are more opted to continue training through the swim, cycle, run, and competition than non-minority parents, increasing the pool of participants in the years to come than in urban communities.

USA Triathlon has engineered the sport of triathlon for youth as early as three years old, ensuring a safe entry into the sport. With parental guidance and access to equitable resources, youth across the country can enjoy a sport that grows with them in age and development. National Governing Bodies such as USA Triathlon, International World Triathlon, and United States Olympic and Paralympics Committee collectively have opportunities for youth to grow up and through the sport until the ripe young age of choice with the right certified coach leading the way.

Certified Triathlon Coaching Opportunities

USA Triathlon

1. Youth & Junior
2. Youth and Junior ELITE
3. Youth & Junior (High-Performance Team)
4. Level 1 Coach
5. Level 2 Coach
6. Level 2 (Endurance)
7. Level 3

This series of certified coaches can assist in the successful progression of youth into adulthood in the sport of triathlon from #1 to #7; however, there is a distinct difference between a certified tri coach that works with youth and a certified coach that works with adults. Working with adults is different than working with youth and vice versa. Youth and Junior ELITE and High-Performance Coaches are trained differently than coaches that are just Youth and Junior Certified and so forth. While Level 1 and up coaches are provided a baseline in youth development within the sport, the foundational theory of success is not provided for execution. In other words, adult tri coaches (Level1 – Level 3) need certifications in Youth & Junior, Youth & Junior Elite, and High Performance to be successful.

What is important to note is that the success of youth into adulthood through the sport of triathlon is contingent on their access to the listing of certified coaches in the order presented above for increased performance

and decreased injury while still having fun along the way. Learn more about coaching certification levels and opportunities at www.usatriathlon.org.

Recently, Sister Madonna — aka the "Iron Nun," celebrated her 90th birthday and still participates in triathlons (proving age is just a number) and inspires us every day and people everywhere.

The sport of triathlon has limitless potential for youth across the world, but a disparity does exist for youth in underserved and underrepresented communities. Despite this disparity, Dr. Tekemia Dorsey developed an infrastructure that extends beyond the sport of triathlon that leads to tremendous success beyond being an athlete and a medal for urban youth, urban communities, and their urban futures. (See Figure 1.2)

"To say that majorities, as such, have a right to rule minorities, is equivalent to saying that minorities have, and ought to have, no rights, except such as majorities please to allow them."

-Lysander Spooner

BENEFITS OF THE SPORT OF TRIATHLON FOR ADULTS & YOUTH

In September 2017, Kenan Pala released a Blog on the fantastic benefits of triathlon. It is fitting to repost below without having to reinvent the content.

Better physical health

Triathlon is an excellent physical activity that combines cardio buildup, muscle mass increase, and stamina boost. Engaging in triathlons brings down blood pressure, lowers the risk of osteoporosis, and prevents cardiovascular issues and even certain cancers.

Also, triathlon uses different muscles for the different stages. Using different muscles during exercises leads to a complete workout for your entire body (and not just part of it). Cross-Training the body helps keep you strong, not just in one area but also in your entire physical being.

Improved mental health

The distance for a triathlon is longer than most races and requires more athletic skills than most sports. To complete one of these races, you need to have a solid physical side and a tough mental side to convince yourself that you can do it.

Although the races are long in triathlons, a solid mental state helps you go through the challenging stages of the race.

Weight loss

If you are having problems with weight management, the rigorous demand for triathlons will burn off your body fat faster than other conventional exercise routines. And because triathlons are much more fun than running the treadmill or following a strict diet, the results are more long-lasting.

Note, however, that you should not do a full triathlon immediately to lose weight. Ensure that you undergo training and the necessary endurance buildup before signing up for your first triathlon event.

Less risk of injuries

Unlike conventional workouts that tend to focus on specific body parts, the holistic approach of a triathlon distributes the workload to more body parts. As a result, your body will have less likelihood to experience local injury or pain. Compare that to an hour of biking alone, which will drive the pain solely on your legs.

Improved motivation to exercise

Nothing is boring for a triathlon, mainly because you must prepare for three different sports in a single race! As a result, your preparation workout won't be routine. If you plan to develop your swimming today, you can do running tomorrow and then biking the day after that.

Develop multidisciplinary skills

Who says you can only become good in one sport? Triathlons allow you to become the best in all three events – swimming, biking, and running! If you think you are lagging in one of these stages, you can further develop that skill to optimize your entire triathlon.

Best of all, it allows you to develop your character. Despite the physical challenges of the three stages, pushing through and finishing the triathlon gives you a sense of accomplishment through sheer determination and dedication.

Inspire others

The toughness of doing a triathlon is no joke, and so when people see that you can do it, it might prompt them they too can accomplish the completion of a triathlon. As you put your effort and boldness to finish a triathlon, this will create a naturally inspiring story for people to lead them towards aiming for better health and achieving the (seemingly) impossible.

BENEFITS OF THE SPORT OF TRIATHLON FOR URBAN YOUTH

The benefits of the sport of triathlon for urban youth have similarities with youth from suburban and rural communities, and then there are distinct differences. Similarities include those captured in the previous section, such as better physical health, improved mental health, less risk of injuries, weight loss, improved motivation to exercise, development of multidisciplinary skills, and inspiration to others. The disparity of the sport is not just rooted within the sport of triathlon but also external to the sport itself. The disparity is defined as a lack of similarity or equality; inequality; difference, such as disparity in family makeup; disparity inequitable resources, etc.

Distinct differences rooted within the sport of triathlon and external of the sport assist in the barriers and benefits of the sport for urban youth, urban communities, and their urban futures. The disparity is a huge concern in life and the sport of triathlon as it relates to urban youth, urban communities, and increasing participation in the future. A widespread discussion in the triathlon industry is that of privilege. Privilege is defined as "a special right, advantage, or immunity granted or available only to a particular person or group. Privilege is not a word synonymous with urban communities, but disparity it is.

The benefits of the sport of triathlon for urban youth and urban communities remain the "untapped potential" the sport has and a leader's vision to connect the dots for maximum exposure. The sport of triathlon offers youth, regardless of disparity (lived, inherited, or faced), opportunities beyond what single-disciplined sports offer. For example, the youth of varying sizes, ages, socioeconomic and geographic backgrounds, etc., join track and field clubs; however, only those who already have the "talent and next-level potential" are provided are embraced and nurtured for exposure. Like track and field, football has the same impact on youth in attracting large numbers to tryouts. Trying out and exhibiting an interest does not elude being picked to step on the field for more than adequate playing time or one or two plays. Youth are sidelined during football games and only the best of the best dominates playing time.

The rise of obesity across the country is primarily contributed to the lack of youth engaged in physical activity they have or expressed an interest in and not chosen or felt they were less than capable of taking part. Neither of these scenarios matters in the triathlon sport because every youth who shows up can participate. The applicability of the triathlon sport to all is the primary reason it is apart from any other sport (single or multisport).

The Parallel Chart of Opportunity through the Sport of Triathlon for Urban Youth, Urban Communities and their Urban Futures is Brainchild by Dr. Tekemia Dorsey (CEO, Executive Director, The International Association of Black Triathletes; Senior Consultant – DTD Urban Multisport Consulting Firm)

Dr. Tekemia Dorsey's Infrastructure Model for Urban Youth, Urban Communities, and Their Urban Futures can be adapted to any sports discipline that has a progression of growth and development, such as the USA Triathlon.

Dr. Dorsey has been able to connect the sport of triathlon in areas of life that matter to all but especially in urban communities, such as education, workforce development, college, and career exploration, jobs and internships, leadership training and development, personal and professional development, academic, health and mental enrichment.

Dr. Dorsey has been able to connect the sport of triathlon in areas of life.

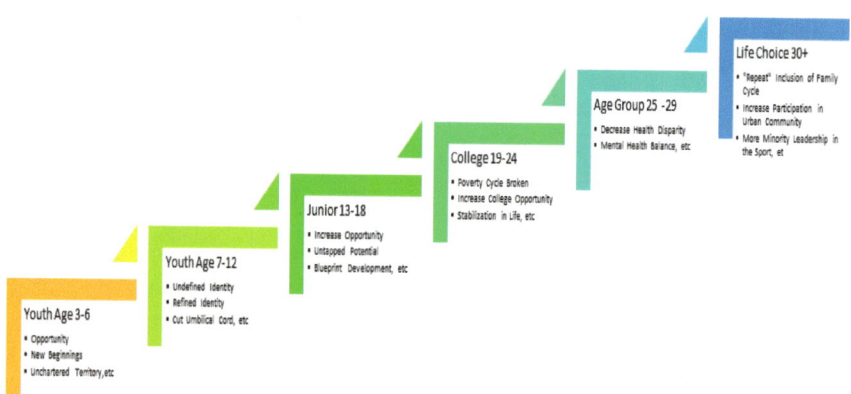

That matters to all, especially in urban communities, such as education, workforce development, college and career exploration, jobs and internships, leadership training and development, personal and professional development, academic, health, and mental enrichment.

Youth Ages 3-6
•Opportunity, New Beginnings, Unchartered Territory, etc

In urban communities, youth ages 3-6 years old do not automatically have equal access to resources such as pools or parents interested in the triathlon sport versus simply using the sport as an activity. The triathlon sport is a way of engagement for youth in this age category. For youth ages 3-6 years old, the triathlon sport shifts from just taking part in a sport and earning a medal to an opportunity to new beginnings and unchartered territory that led to more later in life.

When one thinks of the family dynamics of an urban family, it is quite different from that of families in suburban and rural areas. Most urban family dynamics may comprise single parents, grandparents, aunts and uncles, homelessness, and even foster care instead of other community makeups (suburban and rural).

Access to resources (equitable) or not is different for youth in urban communities. Most believe that pools are the core of a lack of why youth are not in the sport of triathlon, and that is not even at the surface of known, assumed, and uncertain barriers for urban youth.

Other barriers that exist include but are not limited to transportation, family support, family dynamics, money, time, interest, equipment, safe areas to train, increased crime rate and violence, exposure, awareness, education, opportunity, and leadership).

Despite the significant barriers and disparity in urban, rural, and suburban areas, youth exposed to the sport of triathlon at the age of 3-6 years of age notably benefit far more significantly than youth exposed to the sport later in life. Youth in this category of life is fearless, resilient, optimistic, energetic, and intrigued with the unknown. The sport of triathlon assists in building their confidence, sense of self, sense of excitement, sense of independence, sense of critical and logical thinking, sense of improved communication, sense of maturity, sense of family, but mainly a sense of achievement.

It is a proven fact when one review the data on the number of youth in the sport of triathlon or minorities overall, youth from urban communities are underrepresented. A Certified Youth and Junior Tri Coach could assist in the firm foundation of youth from any background in the sport of triathlon worldwide.

Youth Ages 7-12
•Undefined Identity, Refined Identity, Cut Umbilical Cord, etc

In urban communities, youth in the category of 7-12 years old are introduced to the sport of triathlon, able to overcome some of the barriers from category 3-6 years old, continue to benefit from the personal growth and development that sports can impose on a young life. Benefits include but are not limited to tapping an undefined identity, a redefined identity, the cutting of the umbilical cord from parents, etc.

Although sports can provide a strong foundation for youth, what continues to nurture and manifest greatness for youth through sports, especially in the triathlon sport, is the leadership of a Coach with a vision and mission that connects the dots. Growing up in different communities (suburban, rural, and urban) evoke different ethics, morals, and values within youth and families. It is not rocket science nor a negative review of one versus the other; communities are what they are and those that live in them.

Well-known facts show that those living in urban communities do not come from wealth or abundant resources and opportunities. In contrast, those from rural and suburban communities are considered more privileged. Creating pathways for success for diverse populations is a missed opportunity for those in influential positions working in suburban and rural communities.

What separates the progression of youth in life are the type of leadership their coach embodies and their ability and aspiration to connect the dots beyond the sport. While every sport has roadblocks, internal and external barriers must be acknowledged and addressed for the athlete's good, families, communities, and future endeavors. In this case, the barriers discussed are the sport of triathlon, suburban and rural versus urban communities, certified triathlon coaching opportunities, the coach's leadership characteristics, and their ability to connect the dots.

Urban communities lack an understanding that triathletes, especially those of color, exist and understand the triathlon sport itself. Persons living in urban communities lack education about the sport, awareness of the sport, certified coaches, and coaching opportunities to expose youth to the sport, so when a black certified triathlon coach exists in an urban community, efforts for change must be presented. Knowledge is not impactful if the one that possesses it keeps it for the benefit of self-versus its community.

A lack of representation in coaches, race directors, and clubs from urban communities remains a barrier to growth and development in the triathlon sport. Although these are barriers to success, success still exists noteworthy of sharing and replication.

In urban communities, youth between the ages of 7-and 12 face a pivotal period in their lives on many levels. In terms of sports, urban youth in this age range either progress forward or stagnate as an athlete in single disciplined sports; however, in the sport of triathlon, youth are still progressing and developing their talents and understanding their potential.

In the sport of triathlon, youth ages 7-12 would still benefit from the expertise of a Certified Youth and Junior TRI Coach, and some would begin to pique the interest of a Certified Youth and Junior ELITE Coach. In the sport of triathlon, as youth show potential in their respective disciplines and interest in growing to the next level, the next progression could include the ELITE pathway as an option. Through the sport of triathlon under USAT's model, as youth grow in skill and development, so do their potential in the sport itself through college. Still, since there is a lack of opportunity in the sport of triathlon in urban communities, urban youth lack the opportunity for growth and development (college and career, etc.).

Although youth in the sport of triathlon can grow in the sport through age, skill, and development (if exposure and opportunity exist) with a Certified Youth and Junior TRI Coach like in single-disciplined sports, the million-dollar question often asked is, "What is available for them beyond the sport?" Additionally, "What is the linkage to keep the youth interested in future development and opportunity within the sport?" These questions are essential for youth to create buy-in for continuation. Dr. Tekemia Dorsey has been able to answer the question from a more extensive view beyond the sport of triathlon itself. It is worth noting that there is a long-term opportunity leading to college in the sport of triathlon. Still, the gap exists in connecting the puzzle pieces for the general audience to understand and embrace.

Junior 13-18
•Increase Opportunity, Untapped Potential, Blueprint Development, etc

In the sport of triathlon, when youth enter the age group of 13 and beyond, they have three unique pathways to consider before college:

1. Youth & Junior (based on age and skill development, based on continued interests in the sport)

2. Youth & Junior Elite (based on advanced skill and recommendation from a Certified Youth and Junior Elite Coach. In this pathway, their racing circuit changes, and there is an opportunity to be scouted for USAT Development Team??)

3. High School Club/Team (based on age and level of education that extends from the normal Youth & Junior Pathway and the Youth & Junior Elite Pathway, youth can compete at the high school level).

Note: Youth that follows the Youth & Junior ELITE pathway when they enter the age of high school can defray from that pathway and return to regular racing on the high school level (if one exists in their area).

In urban communities, these options are not as familiar to urban youth widespread simply because of a lack of education, a lack of awareness, and a lack of exposure. Pockets of urban youth across the country may be familiar with the triathlon sport through media such as video or participating in competition/events but not enough to start a trend or impact growth. The lack of education, awareness, and engagement of urban youth in the triathlon sport remains a concern. The lack of education, awareness, and exposure is because of a lack of representation through black coaches, black race directors, and black triathletes (adult and youth).

Urban communities lack opportunities for growth and development because there have not been any coaching certification opportunities hosted in urban communities. Historically Black Colleges and Universities (HBCU) lack familiarity with the triathlon sport, have USA Triathlon Collegiate Club Programs, NCAA Women Varsity Triathlon Programs, USAT Intern Programs, or pathway opportunities for urban youth to take advantage of directly related to HBCUs.

There are no Private White Institutions (PWI's) that have initiatives to attract urban youth from urban communities to their triathlon programs, such as NCAA, Collegiate Club, etc., which remain an even more considerable disparity. Around PWI's and HBCUs, there is a lack of grassroots initiatives (programs – education, awareness, and exposure) around the thirty-seven college/universities that currently offer triathlon programs for urban youth, urban communities, and their urban futures.

Urban youth from urban communities remain at a disadvantage at this stage in the age group 13-18 in the sport of triathlon compared to youth from rural and suburban communities.

For youth from rural and suburban communities, there is a blueprint of success that led to high school and collegiate opportunities. Still, a blueprint is lacking for urban youth from college/universities, national governing bodies, etc. For youth in urban communities, the sport of triathlon provides untapped potential and untapped opportunities that have not been developed until now by Dr. Tekemia Dorsey, The International Association of Black Triathletes, and the IABT Junior Multisport Club.

Collegiate 19-24
•Poverty Cycle Broken, Increase College Opportunity, Stabilization in Life, etc

In the sport of triathlon, opportunities continue for rural and suburban youth through college and beyond collegiate endeavors. These opportunities include USA Triathlon Collegiate Club, NCAA Women's Triathlon Programs, triathlon intern opportunities, and Age Group progression once the collegiate competition concludes. Even if youth have opportunities to race and compete on the collegiate level (later age group), those from rural and suburban communities have a unique opportunity instead of youth from urban youth. The advantages youth from suburban and rural communities have cross-trained in swimming, cycling, and running to decrease health disparities and increase family bonding and participation, increasing the cycle of life in the sport with siblings, etc.

In urban communities, youth lack opportunities to college outside the sport of triathlon but would gain an advantage in college if exposed to the sport of triathlon early on, like youth from rural and suburban communities. For youth from urban communities, the sport of triathlon provides multiple alternative pathways to college, such as triathlon, swimming, running, academic and scholarship, to name a few. The sport of triathlon in urban communities for youth can assist in breaking the cycle of poverty, somewhat stabilize life, increase college, career, and internship opportunities, and the list continues.

Age Group 25 -29
•Decrease Health Disparity, Mental Health Balance, etc

As youth transition into an asset to society, those that take part in the triathlon sport have an unwavering advantage over those that do not take part in the triathlon sport. At this stage in life, youth from suburban and rural communities embark upon new creative and innovative opportunities the sport presents. Those from suburban and rural communities have opportunities such as still competing, becoming coaches, launching, or positively contributing to programs from which they derive, growing and expanding the sport, introducing the sport to siblings and others within their communities, and having a new way and outlook on life.

At this stage in the sport, young adults are still racing and competing, those from rural and suburban communities anyway. They are simply in a better place than those from urban communities. If more youth from urban communities were involved in the sport of triathlon at this stage of life and grew up in the cycle of progression as their rural and urban counterparts, urban youth would be better mentally and physically. Urban youth would experience a significant shift in decreasing health disparities as well.

Life Choice 30+
• "Repeat" Inclusion of Family Cycle, Increase Participation in Urban Community, More Minority Leadership in the sport, etc

It remains a known fact that the triathlon sport continues to grow because those who grew up in and through the sport will most likely give back, grow and expand the initiative, and get more family and friends involved beyond the age of thirty. However, with the lack of equity and diversity in the sport in the thirty-age group and younger, minorities lack advantages to cycle through the triathlon funnel. Minorities' lack of advantages to cycle through the triathlon funnel will result in a legacy of transformational change for urban youth and their future endeavors. Fewer minorities will reach the thirty-age group, reducing other minorities having grown in and through the sport, having the same playing field to give back, grow and expand the initiative, and get more family and friends involved beyond the age of thirty.

THE IMPACT THE SPORT OF TRIATHLON COULD HAVE IN URBAN COMMUNITIES

The impact of the sport of triathlon on youth from rural and suburban communities is clear and has been clear for years. It is clear from those in leadership positions and positions of influence that they devise coaching education, programs, events, pathways, or attempts in development pathways, and the list continues. It is clear from those in leadership positions and positions of influence because when initiatives to date have been discussed and developed, urban youth, urban communities, and their urban futures were not part of the discussion or at least part of the discussion with a more realistic outcome.

In the next section, "A Deep Dive" is presented in understanding how the sport of triathlon can and has had on urban communities, urban youth, and their urban futures from the experiences, knowledge acquisition, trials and tribulations with successes and drawbacks, etc. from those living in urban communities. More is needed to make the targeted population of urban youth and urban communities a priority for positive change in inclusion in the years to come.

One can advocate that when is in a position of leadership and influence, one should surround oneself and develop a strategic plan of change to ensure there is an impact that represents all persons of the world if that is the organization's intent. Although the impact is not as significant as possible, more is expected now that knowledge and processes have been shared.

A leader is one who sees more than others see, who sees farther than others see and who sees before others see."

Leroy Elmes

DISPARITY IN PROGRESSION BETWEEN CULTURES IN THE SPORT OF TRIATHLON

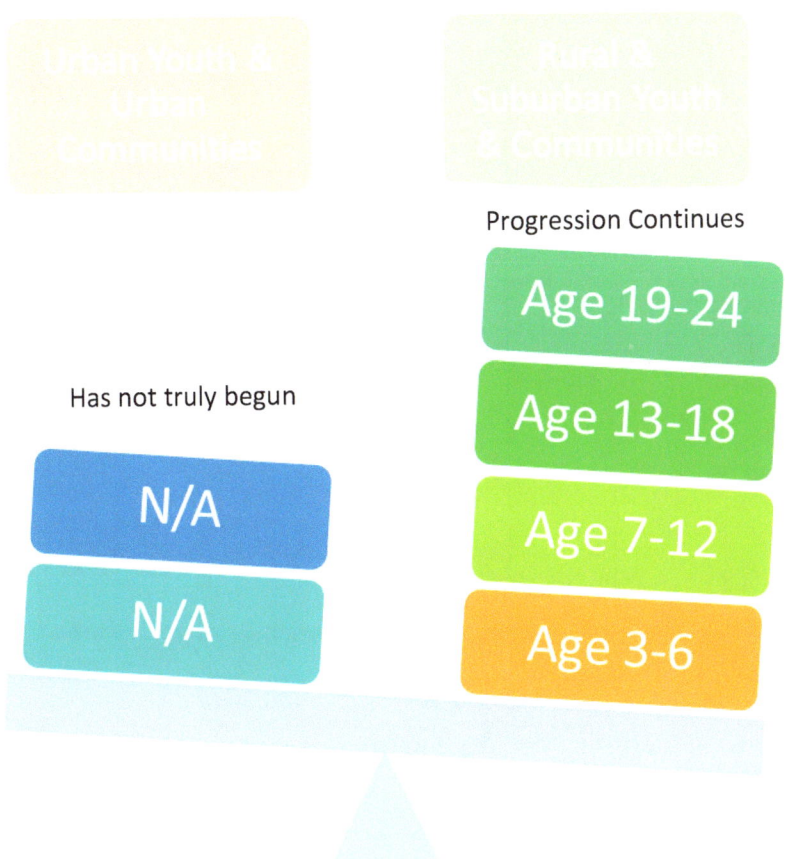

Unlike single-disciplined sports, the multisport industry provides a different angle for success if implemented through the right visionary leaders' lens. The variables and barriers impacting urban youth, urban families, and urban communities are essential to know and understand before attempting change for success. The multisport industry is no different.

Around the globe, coaches wonder how to integrate success off the field with success on the field. Educators attempt to connect the dots academically with non-athletes and academically with athletes in education. Gaps remain in both populations.

In single discipline sports, youth in urban communities look for time on the field to escape, ways to increase activity, and even ways to create a better future. However, statistics show that a small percentage of youth make it to college or the pros. They must be highly skilled.

There is a lack of education, exposure, and participation in the sport for youth in urban communities in the multisport industry. Coaching is the slightest worry of coaches in the sport until more increased opportunities surface for urban youth.

In education, youth in urban communities aspire to college and be successful in life. Although attending college remains a goal, unfortunately, few can achieve their dream successfully.

To date, organizations continue to have a single lens throughout the world regarding sports, education, and post-secondary/career connections. It is either one or the other, not a culmination.

What if there was a way to close sports, academic, and college/career gaps under one organizational roof?

Is that even possible, you ask? Yes, it is.

What are topics close to urban communities that could impact growth and development for youth and their families?

Topics such as finances, transportation, access to resources, gaps in educational opportunities outside of the school system, gaps in training, parental/guardian level education, training, life's navigation, and the list continues.

These topics are not even at the root cause of concerns in urban communities that prevent urban youth success. However, often a solution arises that can connect the dots and a pathway toward positive change.

Using the multisport industry as a foundation, Dr. Tekemia Dorsey has connected the dots and created a pathway toward positive change for urban youth, including sports, education, workforce development, college, and career readiness, and more.

Getting people to grasp comprehensive concepts is tricky because it is not the norm. As humans, people tend to wrap their heads about simple first and complex later or never.

That is ok because life is not as simple as we would like and is very comprehensive in navigation.

Dr. Tekemia Dorsey has clarified the complexity of barriers and concerns for youth and families in urban communities, only using the triathlon sport as a base for success.

IABT Junior Multisport Club & Dr. Tekemia Dorsey's Sports Academy 4 Urban Youth

For rural and suburban youth, the sport of triathlon gives privilege not afforded to urban youth. For rural, suburban, and even urban youth, the triathlon sport provides a pathway to collegiate and career opportunities; however, the path is not as crystal clear as one would have hoped in the sport for urban youth. While the pathway not being crystal clear is not ideal, it is ok.

Dr. Dorsey says that it is ok because the sport lends credence beyond just a medal and training; however, it isn't the idea of a concept that changes lives; it is how the image is cultivated to its fullest potential that matters most.

Dr. Dorsey has utilized the triathlon sport as a part of a larger model that lends value to urban youth, communities, and their urban futures. Value in terms of barriers and concerns not unique to urban communities but obstacles and circumstances that hinder growth and prosperity in life.

Did you know that most of its families live below the poverty line in urban communities? Did you know that the top three categories of those living below the poverty levels are:

1. Females ages 24 - 35
2. Females ages 18 - 24, and
3. Males ages 18 - 24?

Did you know that according to The Governor's Office of Children's website (2020), Maryland's youth unemployment rate is more than three times that of its adult unemployment rate (4.9%), and the number of 16- to 24-year-olds who are unemployed jumped following the recession?

Did you know that the factors contributing to health disparities are complex, interact with each other, and are multi-factorial? Factors include but are not limited to tobacco use, alcohol intake, environmental exposures, family history, lack of quality health care has, racial differences in treatment of disease; poor health-seeking behaviors, such as delays in seeking diagnosis or treatment, or overuse of emergency departments; and lack of health care resources.

In addition to living below the poverty level, facing unemployment, health crises, and access to quality health care, barriers facing urban communities, especially youth, includes a lack of quality programming. More is required for quality programming that provides enrichment opportunities that close the disparity gaps faced by urban youth. Enrichment opportunities such as exposure to preventative education, awareness, and programming versus intervention and postvention services are needed. They need to know that knowledge is POWER.

Prevention vs. Intervention and Postvention Efforts

During Dorsey's doctoral studies in 2005, she developed a secular leadership model centered around youth. In 2006, Dorsey adapted her temporal leadership model to include a non-secular model centered on leadership and youth. Before entering her doctoral studies as a Certified School Counselor, Dorsey implemented her leadership model early in 1997.

Dorsey's Leadership Model is founded on a theoretical/conceptual framework. Dorsey developed two leadership models (17 years ago) (one secular and one non-secular) from which her programming is grounded. These models were developed from the successful completion of her doctoral studies.

Dr. Dorsey's programming provides an approach to prevention versus intervention or postvention efforts, which tend to be too late in urban communities. In urban cities, urban youth do not evolve from privilege, but they will elevate when given opportunities. Dorsey's Leadership Model is a prevention model that intertwines various concepts for success.

After 14 years of implementing bits and pieces of the model in programs with urban youth populations, amid the Covid19 Pandemic, she was able to bring everything together, adding credibility to her model but let's explore a few Case Studies from the last six years that set the foundation of the triathlon sport on urban youth....

Dr. Tekemia Dorsey's Leadership Training & Education Models (Secular & Non-Secular)

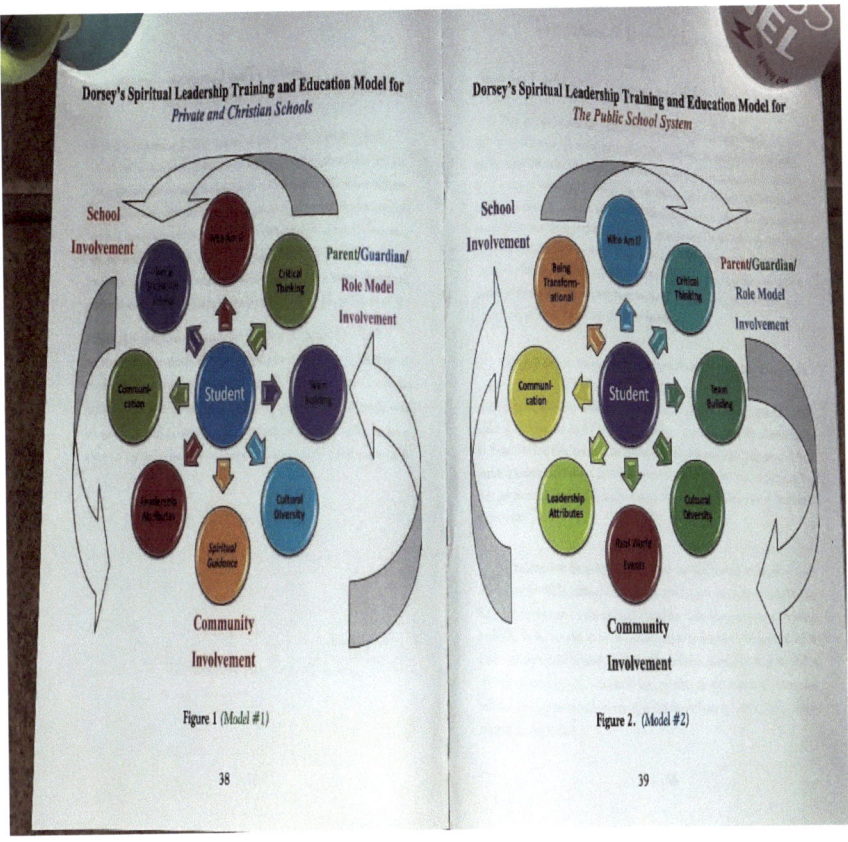

Copyright 2006 @ Dr. Tekemia Dorsey

Leaders. "A leader is one who knows the way, goes the way and shows the way."

—John C.

CASE STUDIES

THE FUTURE OF THE URBAN TRIATHLON SPORT

Dear Future and Aspiring Triathletes,

My name is Halee Simons. How are you doing today? I can remember when I was very new to triathlons. I can remember when I first started out doing triathlons. I was very nervous. I knew I wanted to do it, but I never had the courage in myself to do anything or DO IT. Six years ago, I wasn't confident in myself, and I wanted to run away from things and never step up or own them. If I could tell myself six years ago, it would be, "Halee, you are going to do many things. You will be something great one day; your passion and determination will make something great of you one day. You have to keep on fighting; you are going to make a GREAT and BIG impact one day." To my future and inspiring triathletes, you are about to embark on something that would change your lives forever, IF you chose to follow that path. I chose to do triathlons. One because I wanted to be active in the sport, and two, I knew I wanted to make a difference in the sport. "Halee, what do you mean by that?"

Well, when I first started doing triathlons, I did not know what I was getting myself into at that moment but, once I had completed my first triathlon, I felt a sense of accomplishment in myself when I crossed that finish line. And once I crossed that finish line, I knew that I could do more because that sense of encouragement and crossing that finish line helped me. I know this Virtual Event will seem quite different, but first experiences are never easy, but they are never hard as well! You have to put yourself forward and get through this Virtual Event! Don't you worry, I will be cheering alongside you! Going through this Virtual Event will be a new and learning experience for you guys and this will be a new one for me too. I've never campaigned for a Virtual Event OR even see a virtual event happen, however I, I know that this will be great!

Just some advice that I would give to you will is

a. Make sure you are hydrated

b. Make sure you are eating right. Try not to eat AS much junk food because that can mess up your stomach and make you sick.

c. Make sure you stay focus

d. Get a good night's rest and more importantly,

e. HAVE FUN!

You will be hearing from me again soon but until then! Have fun and stay safe!

Sincerely,
Halee, Scholar Triathlete
IABT Junior Multisport Club Co-Founder

Dear Reader,

Over these last few years, I have grown, not just as an African American or someone with a disability, but as a person. It would be cool to go back in time to see my old self, to talk to him and stuff like that, and share all the things that he is going to do in the future. In the first pages of our book, my mom was explaining the birth of the IABT Junior Multisport Club, and to this day, I always asked myself "What would have happened if I and my sisters never saw our mom compete in Ironman Maryland?" "What if our mom didn't even do triathlons in the first place?" These questions have always been in the back of my head and will always be. But all the things that I've improved on and all the things I have done over these past 6 years were from our mom competing. Also, these things have led me to have confidence, motivation, and the determination to do everything that I've done these past years. I remember before I started doing triathlons, I was really shy and I did not dare to do anything, but when I saw our mom, it motivated me.

One thing that I want you to take away from this book is to stay determined and be motivated; find something that motivates you. There might be some struggles that are difficult for you to accomplish/succeed, and you might want to give up, but if you just hold on to hope and keep pushing through, there will be positive things waiting for you at the end of the road.

Beloved J, Scholar Triathlete
IABT Junior Multisport Club Co-Founder

Leaders lead but in the end, it's the people who deliver that have the greatest impact."

-Tony Blair

LEADERSHIP

How triathlons have made me a leader in my community have taught me how to step up as a leader. It has taught me how to help others in need of my help; it has also taught me how to be a role model for other people. Being a leader in a community, you are always being watched continuously over your shoulder. The way you speak, your image, your behavior, and everything. People are always looking at your maturity level. If you are acting like a kid being 14, people are not going to respect you as a leader, and they won't listen to you either. Doing triathlons and being a part of the triathlon family and community has helped me a lot, and I know it will continue to help with my image and behavior.

Through triathlons I quickly learned that people needed and wanted to be treated equally. No one wants to be treated like they are under someone, or even feel like they are being treated less than equally or anything! Learning that from triathlons, I have been able to use my abilities and skill sets to help change that for my community. For example, during the summer, my cohort and I did three TRIAD Initiatives.

The first TRIAD Initiative was the Hat, Coat, and Glove Drive, where we donated clothes to underserved and underrepresented youth and families. Our 2nd TRIAD Initiative was the Virtual 5k Run/Walk Event where you run or walk your 5k, and then you would record time and upload it to the IABT's website. Our 3rd TRIAD Initiative was the Health and Wellness Event, where we prepared and distributed to participants to get swag bags that included a Mental Health Bag, Planner, a Snack Bag and other goodies. They also did a mini-1-mile run/ walk and at the end, my cohort and I received student service-learning hours. I completed each of these three TRIAD Initiatives with my cohort and it felt great.

Halee, Scholar Triathlete
IABT Junior Multisport Club Co-Founder

Triathlons have helped me become a better leader in a lot of different ways. It helped me feel more comfortable when I do active things around my community such as doing fundraisers for urban communities, getting others involved in the sport, and so much more! I have a disability, and my disability is called a neurological tick disorder where parts of body and limbs act up.

Being a leader when I have a disability has a greater impact for what I do because all the struggles that these physically challenged youth have been through, I have been through the same thing as well so I know how they feel, and I can have a better connection with them. When I started triathlons, I felt really alone because I thought that I was the only one that had a disability in the sport of triathlon, but later in my experience with triathlons, I have seen more people in the multisport industry that is physically challenged, so I feel like I am in a pack in triathlons. I have grown as a person to have the courage and the dedication to lead.

Beloved J, Scholar Triathlete
IABT Junior Multisport Club Co-Founder

PERSONAL GRATIFICATION FROM THE SPORT

When I started the sport of triathlon, I knew what it did for me. Engaging in the triathlon sport allowed me to overcome something that was on my bucket list, and that was learning how to swim, and then it became training, competing, and becoming an Ironman. Already having 25 years of running and a few years of cycling (casually) under my belt, swimming remained the weak link and key to success. Although learning to sit on my trainer for cycling was another whole level of experience, I quickly had to adapt. Cycle training on a trainer helped with a new mental attitude towards success. Swimming was what I had to learn to overcome, and to this day, it was self-gratifying accomplishing that goal. I was able to go from non-swimmer to Ironman in 9 months and 15 days.

While training for Ironman, Maryland, in 2014, I had four children at home (three young), watching me train and overcome these hurdles within myself. I had one that was getting ready to finish high school and three young ones in elementary school. The three in elementary school were watching me day in and day out, watching me spending hours on my trainer in my business room on the weekends, watching and listening to Netflix movies, trying to balance this thing called nutrition every 30 minutes. These times did not include getting up and going to the pool five to six days a week to train in swimming, so I would not drown during the event.

After I completed Ironman Maryland in September 2014, that October 2014, they said, "We want to do a triathlon and be a triathlete like you."

I said, "Are you sure?" They said, "Yeah. We want to do what you do." I had no idea that they were watching me. I said, okay, being a coach for about 22 years at that point, the only background I was not as comfortable with was swimming, so I decided to apply what I knew from my training until I had the chance to become a Certified Swim Coach.

Their first training began in October 2014 when I started training the three of them together, and over the next few weeks, by Thanksgiving, two of the three were swimming across the length of the pool (my oldest girl [Heaven] and my youngest son [BJ]). They were elated. My middle child and youngest daughter (Halee) took a while longer, but it was well worth it for her.

We were already running as a family about five-seven miles every other weekend the spring before and during the summer, so running was not a big deal. They had engaged and excelled in sports before learning how to swim, such as cheerleading, t-ball, softball, football, and dance. They were already athletes, but now they are breaking into a sport that remained taboo, which included first learning how to swim.

Dr. Tekemia Dorsey

THE BIRTHING OF THE
IABT JUNIOR MULTISPORT CLUB

They continued to progress in swimming over the next six months and took part in their first multisport event in April 2015.

Two months later, they engaged in their second multisport event and first triathlon event in June 2015. I have seen adults involved in multisport events but never youth. It is one thing training, and there is another thing competing, and to see them absorb and then demonstrate months of training in an "unknown area" to them and succeed was mind-blowing. My youngest son was learning to live with a neurological tick disorder, and here he did not allow the disability to hold him back from success in this new unknown sport known as triathlons.

In their first season in the sport of triathlon, they took part in roughly six to seven events. They were having fun, enjoying the competition, and progressing as individuals and as siblings through the triathlon sport. The sport of triathlon strengthened their relationships and bonding as siblings. When challenged to do two back-to-back events on any given weekend; collectively, they rosed to the challenge. They competed, completed, and while tired, they were on top of the world.

Throughout their first season in the sport, they were the only three black or minority youth in attendance, outside of some Asian or Hispanic youth here and there. What was surprising, exciting, scary, and uncomfortable in their first season of TRI/DU was that every venue and race was different.

Although the geographic locations and race-day scenarios were quite different, they adapted at such a young age as athletes are required to be successful. A Hagerstown TRI/Du varied differently from a Howard County TRI/Du, different from an Eastern Shore TRI/DU, a Virginia TRI/Du versus a North Carolina TRI/Du, but this did not phase them. The adaptation was remarkable for first-time urban youth in a sport lacking awareness in urban communities worldwide.

Collectively they knew they had trained, and with each event, their confidence grew, and they had each other to lean on and celebrate alongside. The triathlon sport assisted the sibling triathletes in learning the importance of teamwork, leadership, sportsmanship, and an increase in communication skills. There was fear and discomfort again by being the only black/minority youth, but their competitive nature started to show, despite the lack of representation in the sport, which was exciting.

What I started seeing through them was their potential way beyond the sport. They were absorbing the training and executing that training toward each discipline of the triathlon event. By the time we arrived at the races, the primary adjustment was acclimation to the culture of a new venue. It worked because, in their minds, they were hungry to race, excited to compete, getting better with each event while learning self along the way, and remaining goal oriented. They were shooting for the top five and podium slots. It was amazing to witness and experience these youth compete in an unknown and untapped sport for urban youth. Even if they did not achieve their goals for themselves, expectations remained in supporting one another, and that they did. Each race had a pattern, "Get out there; do your best and leave it all there."

By the 2nd to 3rd events, they had begun asking questions. They had begun asking questions I expected to arise one day but not as soon as they had. However, it was made very clear they had discussed with one another before posing the questions to me. The main answer was simple and clear "Where are the other kids that look like me/us?" I was temporarily shocked but decided to answer them as honestly as possible with what knowledge I had acquired to date. My reply was, "There are not many African Americans in the sport, and to date, there is less than 0.05% and even fewer youth, so what you all want to do about it?" They said, well, we want to change that. I suggested forming a club and how they through training, education, and role modeling could make a difference and get more urban youth involved. They liked the concept of starting a club. The IABT Junior Multisport Club was birthed in 2015.

Dr. Tekemia Dorsey

Empowering TRIathletes To LEAD

THE CHANGE IS HERE

Urban youth need to feel accepted. Urban youth need opportunities not normally afforded to them because of their skin color. Urban youth need access to opportunities regardless of their race, gender, ethnicity, socio-economic status, geographic location, family makeup, sexual orientation, disability, academic or athletic prowess. Single focused sports such as football, track and field, tennis, and even cross country have limiters that negatively impact youth. On the contrary, triathlon sports do not have limiters, and youth from any background can engage in training and competition.

The sport of triathlon for urban youth has untapped potential and opportunity for all. The sport of triathlon is more than what urban youth and urban families need now more than ever. Before the Covid19 Pandemic, there were disparities in urban communities needing addressing. Due to the Covid19 Pandemic, the concerns and barriers in urban communities and youth have widened drastically.

Urban youth today are experiencing increases in depression, increased mental health concerns, and an increased need for programs and services that open the doors to addressing solutions vital to success from a foundation of theoretical/conceptual frameworks.

The sport of triathlon has opportunities for urban youth from inception into the sport through collegiate endeavors and beyond. The options that await urban youth through the triathlon sport include collegiate initiatives for females and males.

USA Triathlon created the NCAA Women Varsity Triathlon Program. The NCAA Women Varsity Triathlon Program is now available at 37 colleges/universities with D1, D2, and D3 status.

The pot was sweetened for urban youth when two Historically Black Colleges and Universities adopted the NCAA Women Varsity Triathlon programs.

The USA Triathlon Collegiate Club programs for males and females are also available at more than 60 colleges/universities. With hope, a collegiate club program will be available soon at a Historically Black College and University (HBCU).

Dr. Tekemia Dorsey

"Real leaders are not blinded by the trappings of power but recognize their role as servant."

-Archbishop Desmond Tutu

THE PROBLEM

While these opportunities exist for youth across the country to enter the sport and grow alongside the sport, concerns exist for urban youth. Barriers for urban youth to the triathlon sport do not live with the sport itself; barriers exist with accessibility, education, awareness, exposure, and participation in the sport.

Urban youth have more familiarity with single disciplined sports versus the multisport industry. Due to the lack of urban youth participation in the sport, there remains a disconnect to the collegiate opportunities that await them. How can the gap be lessened in urban communities between the sport and the collegiate opportunities awaiting them?

"You treat people with dignity and respect, and they give it right back to you."

-Bill McDermott

INCREASED OPPORTUNITIES

Dr. Dorsey and IABT and the IABT Junior Multisport Co-Founders (Heaven, Halee, and BJ) introduced the multisport industry to urban communities in 2014. There are opportunities for urban youth to enter the sport in Baltimore City, Baltimore County, Washington, DC, Prince Georges County, Montgomery County, and Brandywine, MD right now. Opportunities for other urban youth remain on the horizon.

The multisport industry is one where the sport provides safe, fun, and exciting introductions, but that is not all. The multisport industry allows individuals such as urban youth to grow with the sport at their desired interest and level, which leads to collegiate opportunities. The reality of attending a college or university is not always as apparent to urban youth as to non-urban youth.

The multisport industry is unique for urban youth with collegiate aspirations, and an out-of-the-box opportunity is needed. For an urban youth to compete on the collegiate level in an NCAA Women's Varsity Triathlon Program or Collegiate Club program is equivalent for minorities applying to Harvard, Yale, Princeton, or other ivy-league schools.

The IABT Junior Multisport Club serves youth from all walks of life, ranging from 5 to 17. The IABT Junior Multisport Club is a gateway to NCAA and Collegiate Club TRI opportunities for urban youth.

Halz S. (aka Halee S.) and Beloved J. have grown up in and through triathlons. Their foundation from the sport has afforded them opportunities far beyond the norm for urban youth, which has been not seen to date. Training, racing, and competing in the pool and open water events, locally and in other states, including Youth & Junior National Championships have set them up as candidates for the NCAA Women's Varsity and Collegiate Club TRI pathways in a few years.

Under Dr. Dorsey's model and leadership, Halz S. (aka Halee S.) and Beloved J. have extended the average reach the sport has afforded even those privileged. Beloved J. and Halz S. (aka Halee S.) have launched their businesses and platforms benefiting urban youth in and through the sport of triathlon for urban youth.

Visit www.theiabt.org or Call 443-267-8783

> "Leadership that brings peace is far more courageous than the one which opens fire and goes for war."
>
> -Asthma Jehangir

AN INTERVIEW WITH THE CO-FOUNDERS OF THE IABT JUNIOR MULTISPORT CLUB

Halz S. (aka Halee S.) and Beloved J. are two of the three co-founders of the IABT Junior Multisport Club, and now they are beginning to venture out on their individual platforms while they collectively raise awareness and advocacy through collective platforms. Halz S. (aka Halee S.) is a special young lady who has been breaking, glass ceilings for young African American females worldwide in and through the sport of triathlon for the last six years. She is only 14 years old. Beloved J. is also knocking down barriers in and through the sport of triathlon for African American males with disabilities. Beloved J. LIVES daily with a neurological tick disorder.

My name is Ms. Halee Simons, better known as Halz S. and I am in the ninth grade. I am the owner of Halz S. Enterprises. I am one of the co-founders of the IABT Junior Multisport Club. I am a scholar - triathlete and I have been competing in triathlons for six years now. I am an advocate for urban youth in and through the sport of triathlon.

My name is Beloved Joshua Simons. I am 12 years old. I am seventh grade. I am one of the co-founders of the IABT Junior Multisport Club and I am a scholar -triathlete, who LIVES with a neurological tick disorder daily. I am the owner of Beloved J. Public Speaking Firm. I have competing in triathlons for six years. I am an advocate for urban youth in and through the sport of triathlon.

"Good leadership consists of showing average people how to do the work of superior people."

-John D. Rockefellar

INTRODUCTION

What got you started in the sport of triathlon?

Beloved J: I got started, in triathlons from the inspiration of our mom, Dr. Tekemia Dorsey, the founder and executive director of The International Association of Black Triathletes, after competing in Ironman Maryland.

Halz S: What got me in the sport of triathlon was my mom, Dr. Tekemia Dorsey, when she did her, Ironman in Maryland in 2014. In 2014, we wanted to do she did because we were interested in it. We also noticed that there weren't really many African American youth out there, so me and my siblings started the IABT Junior Multisport Club.

Our 1stMultisport Race - 2015!
#We Nervous!

We hungry and WE DID IT!
#WhooHoo

INSPIRATION

What inspired you to continue to pursue the triathlon sport?

Halz S.: What really got me inspired was my mom when she was doing her Ironman race. An Ironman race is where you compete a certain distance in about 5 to 17 hours. When we saw it (her Ironman Finish) that day, when we were home (watching via the Internet), she was coming down through the finish line, I saw her really working hard, working really hard to keep up her pace, to the last stretch toward her finish. And once she ran through the finish line, she felt really happy and accomplished and I, also as my brother said, we wanted to get that same experience too; to feel like coming, coming down through the finished line, to know that I completed something very good.

> *"Earn your leadership every day."*
>
> -Michael Jordan

MOTIVATION

Beloved J: I got started in triathlons from the inspiration from my mom and when we begin competing, we didn't see a lot of the IABT Junior Multisport Club to increase the participation of African American people that look like us, so we started the IABT Junior Multisport Club to increase the participation of African American youth in the triathlon sport. We also wanted to assist in decreasing health disparities such as childhood obesity by showing African Americans or just urban youth, how to become active through swim, cycling, and run.

1st Annual Overcoming Childhood Obesity Conference w/Local Rec & Park Program – July 2017

1st Annual Overcoming Childhood Obesity Event "Group FINISHERS Photo" w/Local Rec & Park

What motivated you to say, 'Hey, I saw my mom crossed the finish line. I want to have that same feeling. And when you actually got into the sport, why did you continue on"?

Halz S.: The sport helped me to increase my confidence, boost my low self-esteem, and helped me make friends, which led me to have enough confidence to start my own business. As I said earlier, my business is called Halz S. Enterprises and through my company, I continue to help African American youth understand the gateway through the sport.

Halz S.: I also wanted to give them the same experience as us as well.

On stage at Morgan State University at our 1st Youth & Junior TRI Conference EXPO*Event sharing our triathlon experience with urban youth, coaches, single sport athletes and coaches, etc. We had the honor to share the stage with the Secretary of Education - Maryland, RG3's Mom, single sport youth athletes, and fellow youth triathlete from Michigan. We were the first youth triathlete panel formed and that felt good.

RACING WITH A NEUROLOGICAL TICK DISORDER

What's your inspiration? What's keeping you in the sport of triathlon and what have you learned about yourself?

Beloved J: The inspiration is me, living through my life with a disability called a neurological tic disorder. Me competing in the sport of triathlons makes me feel normal in my life. I continue doing triathlons because I wanted to make a difference in the world for African American youth with, or without a disability(ies).

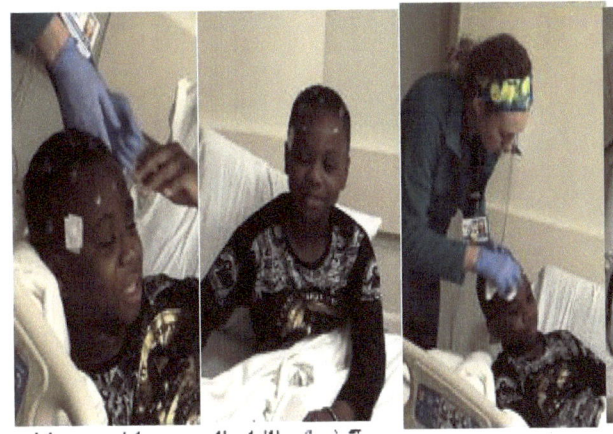
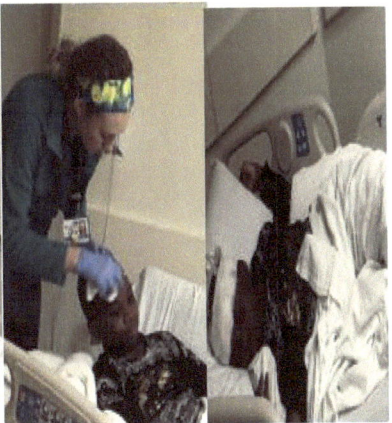

What is a neurological tic disorder? Can you describe it?

Beloved J: A neurological tick order is a disability where parts of your body or limbs act up, and I flinch and twitch up. It affects every part of the body from head to toe. At times, I can have multiple ticks at once; it's very frustrating and at times, I get a little scared.

Dr. Dorsey: And so, living with a neurological tic disorder, would you label yourself with having a disability?

Beloved J: Yes ma'am.

Dr. Dorsey: And how did that make you feel when you realized what was going on with you having a disability in acknowledging being disabled to a degree?

Beloved J: I felt very, disappointed and, very sad because, I didn't want to have this disability in the first place. So,... I was very disappointed about that.

Dr. Dorsey: And so, you went through a period of not being happy with it (having a disability). What actually got you to the point of acceptance?

Beloved J: I actually got to the point of acceptance because of triathlons. When I was competing in triathlons, I felt like I was a part of a group and an awesome community because there were a lot of people that had a disability in the triathlon industry. No one knew or noticed that I had a disability in the first place, so I felt very, happy.

Dr. Dorsey: So, you kind of felt like you were a part of something greater and you could just be who you are?

Beloved J: Yes ma'am, that is correct.

Dr. Dorsey: Now that was self-acceptance. Let's kind of shift for a second as to how did others around you adapt to your ticks, or if they didn't?

Beloved J: I am actually a public speaker, and through my public speaking, I talk to people about my disability and how it helped me through doing the sport of triathlons.

Dr. Dorsey: That's excellent and very inspirational. What grade are you in

right now?

Beloved J: I am in the seventh.

Dr. Dorsey: Alright! So, you know that you are in middle school now, and this is your second year in middle school. Although you accepted yourself in elementary, can you help everyone understand how it was having this disability.

How did it come across to others in elementary and did they come to accept your disability or was there still people that didn't accept it?

Beloved J: There was actually a lot of people that accepted it. So, everyone in my fifth-grade class transferred into the same middle school: Middle River Middle, and all of the people in my classes knew about my disability, but there are some people that came that were new to Middle River Middle. So, I talked to them about, my disability.

Beloved J: At first, they were like "Wait, are you ok?" and "What's wrong with you?". But after I told them about my disability, they were like" Oh, I'm sorry, I didn't know that you had that." And stuff like that.

Dr. Dorsey: So, you were able to vocalize and advocate for yourself by just educating them?

Beloved J: Yes ma'am.

"There is untapped potential in the triathlon sport for urban youth and its part of my/our jobs to enlighten others of the opportunity. That's LEADERSHIP"

- *Beloved J*

BEING AFRICAN AMERICAN & FEMALE

From an African American female perspective, can you describe, *what areas were you having this feeling, that caused you to feel doubt in your head?*

Halz S.: Some areas that made me feel some doubt in myself? I guess I was trying to live up to everyone's expectations because I wanted to seem really happy and joyful, not negative and always encouraging others.

On the inside, I felt like I have myself but on the outside, I was like, this really-half happy, joyful person, but on the inside, I am really battling with my self-esteem and self-confidence. So, I try to not let people see that and only see myself gain confidence.
And I'll always give people advice, like if they have any problems going on but the advice, I give to them, I never give it to myself.

Dr. Dorsey: Okay. So, that's a lot of wisdom from a 14-year-old. It's powerful for you to admit that, you know, you to acknowledge wanting to please others, but inside crying out. You talked about the sport of triathlon helping to build your self-esteem and self-confidence.

How did training or competing help you to feel that pride on the inside to match up with your persona on the outside?

Halz S: How triathlons were

able to help me is that to myself on the outside. I think it was a particular triathlon event where I was dead last, the last one to cross the finish line, which I knew that was okay. To where a point it was ok because as long as I crossed the finish line, "I'm a Winner." And it kind of gave me some boost of motivation just to know that I have to work 10 times harder to not be dead last in my triathlon races. So just knowing that I can at least push myself more to get to my expectations, where I want myself to be.

And so that's powerful because you, you didn't have everyone else to fall back on. You only had yourself.

And so what I'm hearing from you is that, knowing that regardless if you finish first or finish last that you completed the swim, you completed the transition, you completed the bike, you completed the transition again, and then you completed the run. And that, regardless of at this point, you didn't have anyone else to please except Halee. Like that's again, such great wisdom at age 14.

So other young ladies, that are non-minority or from urban communities that are also going through, you know, bouts of self-esteem and self-confidence and and internally struggling and fighting, but still trying to please others on the outside.

what message would you share for them?

Halz S.: A message I would share for them to keep going, keep pushing on what you're doing, because there's always, even though you're going through a dark tunnel, there's always a light. There's always going to be a bright light at the end of the tunnel.

You just got to keep on fighting, but also

know that you're still learning yourself a little on the way. So, you might have like the best day you ever had during the week. But then immediately after that, like a day later, you might have the worst day you've ever had during the week.

But just knowing just to like take care of yourself, your mental health and your inner self, you can go very far. Just remember that you're still learning yourself along the way, so you may not know whatever's going to happen in the future.

Dr. Dorsey: Do you think that the sport of triathlon could help other African American or non-minority young ladies who might be struggling and if not track along then, what would you recommend?

Halz S.: For young ladies that want to do triathlons, it will definitely help you in, in many ways. It's just like what me and my brother said that triathlons will help you a lot along the way. It will make you learn some things about yourself that you never learned about yourself before.

But if it's ladies who don't do triathlons or don't know who they are, but they have another skill that they want to pursue, to always take advantage, don't be afraid to always, be your own leader in your own field. So, like, say for instance, like any

girls who want to do basketball, like if you really want to do basketball, take charge in that field, in your field of basketball. You need to like wake up early in the morning to practice basketball, and to get on your basketball team at school. It's always a good way to take charge in your field so that you will be successful.

Dr. Dorsey: *So, you saying young ladies must be disciplined, be dedicated and be true to self?*

Halz S.: Yes, absolutely.

"Whether it is a single or a multisport race urban youth are involved in, all they desire is a chance to cross the finish line. In the triathlon sport, we must continue to strive to get more urban youth to the start line first!"
Halz S.

"Growing up the triathlon sport from elem. to high school has afforded me many opportunities, I took advantage of including starting my own business and being featured on local, state and national platforms."
Halz S.

"There is more to me than what you see, I just need people to finally SEE ME than keep on looking pass me even in the triathlon sport"
Halz S.

"I am fearfully and wonderfully made in God's image but my confidence, belief and determination to succeed comes from training and competing in triathlon for the last six years."   *Halz S.*

Junior Elite "Scholar" TRIathlete

Halee Simons
NCAA Women's Varsity Triathlon "HOPEFUL"

BEING AFRICAN AMERICAN & MALE

As an African American male with a disability, did you encounter times of self-esteem and self-confidence along the way and if so, can you help us understand what was that like?

Beloved J: At first, yes, I encountered times of low self-esteem and self-confidence. When I was in fourth grade, I didn't talk about my disability much.

I thought that since I kept twitching, and not a lot of people knew about my disability, I thought that they would look at me differently. I thought that I would look weird and out of place.

Dr. Dorsey: *What would you say to other youth out there that are struggling with a sense of self-esteem or self-confidence or uncertainty?*

When you talked about your earliest segments that triathlon to help you through life, what would you say to them and would you encourage them to get into triathlon?

If not triathlon, what would you inspire them to consider?

Beloved J: The only thing that I would say is use your voice for change. I would say, if you have a disability, use your voice and tell people about what you have. So, they could realize who you are and what you can do. If you want to do triathlons, definitely do it because it's the best sport ever. If you don't want to do it and you want to do a different sport, do it.

I would say that triathlons would be like the most accurate sport to compete in because it has everything that you need to do any sport.

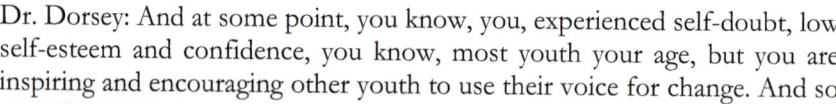

Like if you want to play a sport like football or basketball, swimming, cycling, and running are great disciplines that serves as great cross training for you.

Dr. Dorsey: And at some point, you know, you, experienced self-doubt, low self-esteem and confidence, you know, most youth your age, but you are inspiring and encouraging other youth to use their voice for change. And so that's powerful.

Why are you encouraging youth to use their voice for change? What has that done for you? Why are you encouraging youth to use their voice? What is it about you sharing with others that this triathlon sport helped you feel normal?

Beloved J: Me using my voice has helped me become more of an advocate for myself and others. I no longer have low self-esteem, like I used to have anymore and, I am more confident in myself. I want other youth to have that same feeling and

experience like I did.

Beloved J: I would also say to spread your voice because I do not think that texting or doing anything on social media would make an impact. I would say, going out there and spreading their voice would be a great thing because they will actually get to know you and stuff like that. People actually seeing you talk about what you're doing and actually see what you're going through will go far.

Dr. Dorsey: And by you as a public speaker and you using the topic of sharing the joy of how triathlon has helped you living with a neurological tick disorder, feel normal, do you feel empowered by that? And if so, how?

Beloved J: I do feel empowered by it because I think I can take over the world. I would say that I am empowered because I inspire a lot of people over these years, by my disability.

Empowering TRIathletes To LEAD

"For 5 plus years, I have been an advocate in and through the triathlon sport for urban youth through leadership, community and civic engagement. For my work, I was provided with esteem honor as a 2019 Youth Multisport Philanthropist of the Year Awardee."

Beloved J.

"Life is filled with obstacles and hurdles to jump but it's not what is presented to us, it how we handle them."
Beloved J.

MAKING HISTORY IN THE SPORT

How does it feel to be the first African American youth triathlete turned Business Owner at age 13? How does that resonate for you?

Halz S.: This makes me, feel more and more confident knowing that I accomplished something like this and starting my own business. And knowing that I am working on my future to taking care of myself. So I am not in that poverty level and I am making sure I am working on my future and making sure that I'm not being broke, homeless, or living on the streets. So just knowing that I have a future, a bright future I feel is very accomplished.

Dr. Dorsey: I guess what I want the audience to know is that you don't want to fall into poverty, which happens in a lot in urban communities. If you have to go to a McDonald's or Chick-fil-A or something like that, but working, you just want to make sure you have skillsets, that's gonna encourage your brighter future.

> *"I suppose leadership at one time meant muscles but today it means getting along with people."*
>
> -Mohandas Gandhi

THE LOVE OF THE TRIATHLON SPORT

Halz S.: What I love about the sport of triathlon is meeting different kind of people, races such as white, black, Puerto Rican, Asian, and all the other races. Just to meet those people is really interesting and a great feeling too. It's fun learning about where they come from and stuff like that. So just, just knowing that I am meeting people different races is really nice.

What I also love about the sport or triathlons is that I can compete against other kids ages just like myself, like 14 and up. Competing with them and learning their kind of skill sets and what they've used to learn, like to do to get better, etc. Swimming is really nice as well.

The last thing, what I love about triathlons is that I can potentially go to college on a full ride under the NCAAs women's varsity triathlon program. Beloved J: What I love about the triathlon is that eventually I can compete with people that look like me, just like urban kids, in the sport. I also love that Triathlons can help you go to college on a full ride.

What I also love with the is that now that I'm a public speaker, I can spread the awareness of how triathlons can help other kids with disabilities feel normal and how to help other urban youth others understand how the sport of triathlons can also help their collegiate endeavors.

Dr. Dorsey: You know, and that's powerful that you want to take on these two initiatives, you know, because they've helped you and it's continuing to help others. So, we'll be looking out for you.

Were there any other things that you loved about triathlon that you wanted to add?

Beloved J: Something else that I still love about the sport of triathlons is that I am still potentially learning myself. And that's what I tri for. Me potentially learning about myself through the sport of triathlons is a big steppingstone for myself.

NCAA WOMEN'S VARSITY TRIATHLON PROGRAMS

Dr. Dorsey: Let me pause there for a second, because the NCAA women's varsity triathlon program is a kind of a new movement, originated through USA Triathlon. For the audience who may not have known, the NCAA Women Triathlon Program is in 33-37 colleges/universities, across the US, in Division I, Division II and Division III institutions.

The NCAA Women's Varsity Triathlon Programs are in two HBCU institutions. HBCU means Historically Black College and University. The NCAA Women's Varsity Triathlon Program is powerful for urban youth, like a Halz S, or other African American females from urban communities.

"When you're advocating for something so powerful as the sport of triathlon, you want them to have a clear outlook as to where it can take them"

Dr. Tekemia Dorsey

> *"If people disobey, don't ask what is wrong with them, ask what wrong with their leader."*
>
> -Malcolm Gladwell

AFRICAN AMERICAN FE/MALES - TRI COLLEGIATE CLUB

Dr. Dorsey: Halz S. talked about her potential of getting a scholarship for the NCAA women's varsity triathlon program but for you, it's a little different because although there is not a program for males like the NCAA varsity triathlon program, there are collegiate club programs out there that hopefully by the time you hit college, it may be a full blown program. But for males and females, there are collegiate club programs across the U S that hopefully by the time you get to college and five, four or five years, it may be a full ride. So that's inspiring for you to share not only the collegiate component for you, but I love that last sentence that you said, what was the last sentence?

Beloved J: I can spread the awareness of how triathlons can help other kids with disabilities feeling normal and how to help other urban youth understand the sport of triathlons can also help their collegiate endeavors.

"The task of leadership is not to put greatness into humanity, but to elicit it, for the greatness is already there."

 -John Buchan

PASSING THE TORCH TO THE NEXT GENERATION

1st African American Youth Triathlete Turned Business Owner sounds bizarre and out of this world for a 13-year-old, right? It may sound strange, but I guarantee you it is not.

Halz S., as she is known best in the sport, began training to compete in Fall 2014, alongside her siblings. After her mom completed Ironman Maryland, she and her siblings desired to do the same. They longed to train and do triathlons.

Low and behold, her mom, CEO/Executive Director of The International Associations of Black Triathletes, and now Ironman, Dr. Tekemia Dorsey, became her Triathlon Coach.

In fall 2014, Dr. Dorsey took her three youngest youth to the swimming pool to teach them how to swim. The siblings and Mom had longevity and running and familiarity with cycling. Swimming was the weakest link for the trio of siblings.

Halz S. is the middle child of the trio of siblings and learned to swim last. Her older sister, 18 months older, picked up the concept of swimming first, followed by her younger brother at almost 23 months. Yep, Halz S., as the middle sibling, had the greatest fear of everyone.

Once she revered that fear, she was on her way. She begins to come into her own. Her swim technique surpassed that of her siblings. It was amazing to see these siblings' competitiveness in a sport (swimming) that was new to them. Swimming became a favorite outlet for them and remains such even today.

The triathlon sport consists of three disciplines (swim, cycle, and run) and although swimming was not Halz S.'s most assertive discipline, running and cycling were different animals. Running was the strongest of the three, followed by cycling.

Halz S. in size was on the smaller side compared to her siblings. She was uncertain of her strength, self-esteem, confidence, and ability to excel. These feelings stayed with her for quite a while over the years.

She entered the triathlon sport in elementary school and grew through the sport as she recently started high school. Over the last six years, the triathlon sport has helped Halz S. unveil parts she did not realize she had acquired in single disciplined sports such as softball, dance, or cheerleading.

As training for actual competition grew, a new sense of self emerged with Halz S. A new sense of self, belief, and outlook on life, although a hint of low self-confidence and uncertainty, self-esteem, and comfort in using her voice still existed.

She had blossomed and struggled from elementary to middle school, although she had a few more positive things going for her than before. In elementary school, Halz admitted that she was in the habit of giving others advice and not taking her advice. She also mentioned that she had a habit of pleasing others while masking her internal struggles. These are typical concerns of young females, mostly from urban communities. Halz S. achieved something within herself through the triathlon sport that sparked a difference and initiated a flame that single disciplined sports did not afford her.

Once Halz S. hit Middle School, her confidence and self-esteem began to soar, yet she was still uncertain in some areas. In her personal, athletic, academic, and professional endeavors, there was progress. As a seventh-grader, she had embodied success on and off the field through the triathlon sport.

Success was occurring in the classroom. Success continued in her community through philanthropy and advocacy for urban youth in and through the triathlon sport. She had achieved and excelled as an athlete and coach.

In March 2020, Halz S. debuted her business Halz S. Enterprises, LLC, at the B-More Healthy Expo. She became the first African American Youth turned Business Owner in the world. She has a multitude of accomplishments, such as being the 1st African American Youth Triathlete turned Business Owner, owner of Halz S. Enterprises, Best Selling Author, a scholar-triathlete, co-founder of the IABT Junior Multisport Club, Influencer, Leader, Advocate, swim coach, junior triathlon coach, pioneer, trailblazer, the 2019 Junior Multisport Philanthropist of the Year Award Winner, and recognized by Mayor, County Executives, and Governors for her work on behalf of urban youth in the sport of triathlon.

Halz S. launched her Podcast Show entitled Halz S. Urban Multisport

Radio/Podcast Show in December 2020. Halz S. aspires to earn an entire ride in the NCAA Women's Varsity Triathlon Program, now available at 37 colleges and universities with D1, D2, and D3 schools, including Historically Black Colleges and Universities (HBCUs).

The triathlon sport has untapped potential for urban youth but remains a viable solution. The more urban youth and urban communities become educated and increase awareness, exposure, and access to the triathlon sport, the sky remains the limit on the short-term and long-term impact.

The 2nd African American youth turned business owner with a disability is beginning to sound less weird and more appealing every day. This is beginning to sound less weird to youth that transitioned through IABT's Junior Multisport Club pathways to life.

The youngest sibling trio of the IABT Junior Multisport Club co-founders, Beloved J. business, was birthed during the fourth quarter of 2020 during the covid19 pandemic. Beloved J's business is Beloved J. Public Speaking Firm.

Learn more about programs and services, and to get involved to assist urban youth, urban communities, and their urban futures, visit www.theiabt.org, call 443-267-8783.

Follow us on Social Media:
Facebook: iabtriathletes
Instagram: iabtriathletes
LinkedIn: The International Association of Black Triathletes
Twitter: iabtriathletes

Follow DTD's Urban Multisport Consulting Firm
Website: www.urbanmultisportconsulting.com
Facebook: DTD's Urban Multisport Consulting Firm
Email: info@urbanmultisportconsulting.com

ABOUT THE AUTHORS

Follow Halz S. Enterprises, LLC
Website: www.halzsenterprises.com
Facebook: Halz S. Enterprises
Email: info@halzsenterprises.com

Mister Beloved Joshua Simons owner of Beloved J.'s Public Speaking Firm, a scholar-triathlete, co-founder of the IABT Junior Multisport Club, Best Selling Author, Public Speaker, Leader, Influencer, Advocate, swim coach, junior triathlon coach, pioneer, trailblazer, the 2019 Youth Multisport Philanthropist of the Year Award Winner and recognized by Mayor's, County Executive's and Governor's for his work on behalf of urban youth in the sport of triathlon.

The 1st African American Youth Triathlete turned Business Owner, owner of Halz S. Enterprises, Best Selling Author, a scholar-triathlete, co-founder of the IABT Junior Multisport Club, Influencer, Leader, Advocate, swim coach, junior triathlon coach, pioneer, trailblazer, the 2019 Junior Multisport Philanthropist of the Year Award Winner, and recognized by Mayor's, County Executive's and Governor's for her work on behalf of urban youth in the sport of triathlon, Ms. Halz Simons.

Follow Beloved J Public Speaking Firm
Website: www.belovedjspeaks.org
Facebook: Beloved J Public Speaking Form
Email: info@belovedjspeaks.org

CASE STUDY #2 - DR. TEKEMIA DORSEY'S SPORT ACADEMY 4 URBAN YOUTH

In the spring of 2020, the world faced an unknown pandemic that set programs, organizations, and services back and closed many doors. Yet, Dorsey took the opportunity to gain clarity and shift programming and services for her nonprofit - The International Association of Black Triathletes (IABT). Uncertain of when the opportunity would arise, Dorsey pulled from her archives programming throughout the last few years and created a Hybrid Program from her model.

Throughout April, Dorsey sat, planned, brainstormed, networked, adapted, and finally came up with the program that would be ready to launch once the opportunity arose to do so. Dorsey's plan had two options (1) 100% in-person or (2) Hybrid Program.

In May 2020, unexpectedly and unforeseen, Maryland's Governor Hogan announced that due to the reduction of numbers in covid19 cases, Maryland would be ending Phase 1 on Friday, May 15, 2020, at 5 pm. Due to planning during March and April, Dorsey's plan was ready for action. Dorsey's plan included a distinct group of constituents to engage with from underserved and underrepresented communities.

Partial Press Release Announcement

In a Press Release issued in May, the Headliner says it all, but the first few paragraphs summed up the intent:

The International Association of Black Athletes (IABT) Provides Economic Friendly Summer Hybrid Program for Teens Ages 12 – 16 to Increase Their Marketability, Employability, & Health and Wellness #PostCoVid19 Baltimore, MD.

The International Association of Black Triathletes (IABT) answered the call from County Executive A. Olszewski Jr on May 12 for nonprofits that may have programs and services for Baltimore County residents #PostCoVid19 where relief funds are available via an application process spearheaded by the Baltimore County Foundation. IABT's quest to combat barriers preventing underserved and underrepresented youth and families from success through the sport of triathlon continues, #PostCoVid19.

IABT's Summer Hybrid Program aimed to serve 50 students (middle and high) between 12 – 16 years old residing in under-served and under-represented communities in Baltimore County, Maryland. The dates of the program are June 29 – August 7, 2020. The program has partnered with several organizations to develop a comprehensive, exciting, and engaging plan. The program employs certified instructors where youth will enhance their innate skill set and acquire new knowledge and certifications that will make them one step closer to becoming employable and breaking the cycle of poverty while staying fit.

The design included four (4) components: Leadership Training & Development Through STEM, Workforce Development Education & Certification, Career and College Readiness, and Health and Wellness.

IABT's Summer Hybrid Program had been endorsed by Chairwoman Cathy Bevins, Baltimore County Council, Baltimore County Govt, and Morgan State University.

"Preparation programs for youth are highly needed due to the most recent statistics, and the CoVid19 Pandemic has demonstrated that having degrees and lacking skillsets for adults were not enough to decrease high unemployment rates. Therefore, if we do not change the focus with our youth, those living in poverty will increase sufficiently in the years to come placing youth and families in more despite conditions than CoVid19", says CEO Dr. Tekemia Dorsey.

Although the initial focus was on Baltimore County residents, it soon expanded across Maryland. Dorsey was initially hesitant about the hybrid model because students were forced into online learning from March to the end of the school year. Parents had mixed reviews based on the modality approach (hybrid); however, Dorsey was confident that the program would attract the right set of participants.

Why are these components important?

Leadership Training & Development, Workforce Development Education & Certification, Career, and College Readiness, Health and Wellness, and the newly added component are essential because much is unveiled for success when a dive deep into each is explored. Students do not learn these variables in a program at once. Suppose they become familiar with these topics later in life, such as 11th, 12th, or collegiate years. The latter years are too late to plant seeds and watch them blossom in youth. For youth in urban communities, the later years are too late to learn, explore, and capitalize on these variables for success in life.

PROGRAM BENEFITS OF LEADERSHIP TRAINING AND DEVELOPMENT

All effective youth programs have youth development at their core. Effective youth leadership programs build on solid youth development principles, emphasizing those areas of development and program components that support youth leadership.

IABT's inclusion of leadership development activities as one of the 10 required program elements is consistent with the research (National Research Council and Institute of Medicine, 2002; Gambone, Klem, & Connell, 2002; Sipe, Ma, & Gambone, 1998) showing that effective youth initiatives give young people opportunities to take on new roles and responsibilities through the program and the community.

Most research support facts such as "… that young people need to develop or achieve. In each instance, these competencies or outcomes encompass a wide range of areas such as cognitive, social, civic, cultural, spiritual, vocational, physical, emotional, mental, personal, moral, or intellectual development."

Working definitions include but are not limited to,

1. The ability to lead others or get others to work together toward a common goal or vision (Rutgers Cooperative Extension, 2003; US Department of Health and Human Services, 1996; National Order of the Arrow, 1992; WING SPAN Youth Empowerment Services, n.d.).

2. The ability to lead oneself and work with others while not necessarily influencing others to act (ERIC Clearinghouse on Disabilities and Gifted Education, 1990; Youth Leadership Support Network, n.d.; Urban-Think Tank Institute, 2002; Karnes & Bean, 1997).

3. The ability to guide or direct others on a course of action, influence the opinion and behavior of other people, and show the way by going in advance" (Wehmeyer, Agran, & Hughes, 1998); and

4. The ability to analyze one's strengths and weaknesses, set personal and vocational goals, and have the self-esteem to carry them out. It includes the ability to identify community resources and use them to live independently and establish support networks to participate in community life and to effect positive social change" (Adolescent Employment Readiness Center,

Children's Hospital, n.d.).

Child Trends, a national nonprofit research organization, has compiled an online index of research that demonstrates that youth development programs yield positive outcomes for youth, and IABT's youth programs and services remain at the cutting edge of change in urban youth worldwide.

PROGRAM BENEFITS OF WORKFORCE DEVELOPMENT PROGRAMS

Youth employment remains a global challenge, with an estimated 80 million youth unemployed in low- and middle-income countries worldwide, and numbers are rising. When youth are educated, healthy, employed, and civically engaged, they have the power to drive economic growth, democracy, resilience, and prosperity.

However, when the needs of youth are not addressed, poverty, violence, and unrest can follow. In contexts where lack of skills contributes to high unemployment, workforce development is the practice that targets this challenge and maybe one solution, among others.

What Exactly Is Workforce Development?

Youth workforce development is many things to many actors. Understanding how to program for it begins with knowing what it is. At its core, workforce development seeks to benefit two groups: it enables individuals to acquire the knowledge, skills, and attitudes for gainful employment or improved work performance in a particular trade or occupation. And it provides employers with an effective means to communicate and meet their demand for skills.

The Positive Youth Development (PYD) approach intentionally calls for programs geared to youths' age and developmental stages to build youth assets, focuses on building youth agency, provides a supportive environment, and engages with youth rather than viewing them as passive recipients of workforce programs.

Photo Credit: USAID

A PYD approach recommends activities that:

• build youth's assets such as key soft skills or academic or technical skills and knowledge;

• develop youth agency by helping them set goals, develop their own identities, and build confidence that they can accomplish those goals;

• involve youth in decision-making as programs are designed and implemented;

• link youth to a supportive environment through internships and access to mentors; and

• help parents better support youth as they prepare for their economic futures.

IABT's Workforce Development Program aims to provide a stronger foundation and extension into the lives of our youth and families through the sport of triathlon and approach to economic empowerment

PROGRAM BENEFITS OF MENTORING FOR YOUTH

Mentoring is often one component of a program that involves other elements, such as tutoring or life skills training and coaching. The supportive, healthy relationships formed between mentors and mentees are both immediate and long-term and contribute to a host of benefits for mentors and mentees.

Benefits for youth:

- Increased high school graduation rates

- Lower high school dropout rates

- Healthier relationships and lifestyle choices

- Better attitude about school

- Higher college enrollment rates and higher educational aspirations

- Enhanced self-esteem and self-confidence

- Improved behavior, both at home and at school

- Stronger relationships with parents, teachers, and peers

- Improved interpersonal skills

- Decreased likelihood of initiating drug and alcohol use

There are many reasons parents choose tutoring for their children. Some parents feel unable to help their children with schoolwork. Others may find their children are more receptive to working through school struggles with another person. Tutoring can help strengthen subject comprehension, boost confidence, and build important learning skills.

Tutoring gives students individualized attention that they don't get in a crowded classroom. This helps children who struggle to keep up, as well as those who aren't challenged enough. It also keeps students on track during breaks from school, such as during March Break, or during the summer.

The minimum wage is the teenage black unemployment act. It is the guaranteed way of holding the poor, the minorities and the disenfranchised out of the mainstream is if you price their original services too high.

-Arthur Laffer

PROGRAM BENEFITS OF TUTORING

Tutoring programs can help your child develop study and learning skills that will help set up your child for success for his or her entire life. There are many advantages of tutoring services:

1. **Individual and unique learning experience**: Your child will receive an individualized learning experience he or she can't always get in a classroom setting. Tutors can customize the lessons and activities just for your child.

2. **One-on-one attention**: Tutors get to know your child's individual learning style and can adapt teaching methods accordingly. They act as your child's own private teacher.

3. **Improves academic performance**: Tutoring will prepare your child for tests and exams, while tutors work with your child on specific problem areas. Your child's grades and understanding of the subject will significantly improve when working with a tutor.

4. **Improves attitude towards learning and school**: Learning will become fun for your child. With constant encouragement and praise, your child will no longer feel overwhelmed or frustrated with school.

5. **Encourages self-paced and self-directed learning**: With tutoring, your child will learn to take the initiative his or her schoolwork. Your child will also learn how to control the learning pace.

6. **Improves self-esteem and confidence**: Your child's self-esteem and confidence will increase through tutoring, by providing him or her with the resources and skills he or she needs to excel in school.

7. **Improves work and study habits**: Through tutoring, your child will learn work and study habits he or she will use for life. These skills will help prepare your child to successfully achieve his or her goals both inside and outside of school.

8. **Positive workspace**: Tutoring provides an environment free of distractions, with fewer students and disruptions around so your child is better able to focus on learning.

9. **Encourages independence and responsibility**: Your child will gain the ability to do schoolwork on his or her own, without your help. Your child will realize his or her own personal growth and will learn to take

responsibilities for his or her studies.

10. **Helps overcome learning obstacles**: Your child's tutor will specifically target whichever aspect of learning he or she is having troubles with, whether it's writing, math, language, or reading.

11. **Encourages the freedom to ask questions**: At school, your child may not always feel comfortable asking questions in front of his or her peers. Tutoring will help teach your child to be comfortable asking questions, big or small, without feeling self-conscious.

12. **Improves social and behavioral skills**: Tutoring services will help your child become a better communicator, form better relationships with peers, and make more positive social and behavioral adjustments.

13. **Increases ability to manage one's learning**: Your child will become more competent in his or her learning and more successful in managing his or her schoolwork.

14. **Challenges those who need it**: Tutoring helps bored or under-stimulated children reach their full potential.

15. **Prepares your child for college**: Students heading off to college will learn how to create study plans, develop advanced study skills, and learn superior time management skills. There are numerous benefits of tutoring in college, including reinforcement of existing knowledge and gaining a better understanding of a field of study.

PROGRAM BENEFITS OF CAREER AND COLLEGE READINESS PROGRAMS

College and career readiness programs can provide successful transitions between high school and college or work by helping students gain the skills, knowledge, and expertise needed for their postsecondary success.

• Being college- and career-ready can support students for a lifetime of health in these ways:

• Being prepared for postsecondary education or training that can result in better job opportunities

• Access to a career that provides sustainable wages and pathways to advancement

• Greater income opportunities that support the ability to purchase healthy foods, gain access to physical activity opportunities, and pay for health support services

• Greater social and emotional well-being that comes from having educational and career opportunities and less stress and vulnerability during hard times

"We must not only imagine a better future for women, children, and persecuted minorities; we must work consistently to make it happen - prioritizing humanity, not war."

-*Nadia Murad*

PROGRAM BENEFITS OF HEALTH AND WELLNESS PROGRAMS

High levels of wellbeing in teenagers can help them flourish in life, as well as act as a protective factor against some of the challenges that may arise during the teenage years.

Teenagers with strong mental wellbeing are able to:

- Manage their emotions.
- Enjoy positive relationships with friends and family

"If more stories are told about marginalized communities, subcultures, and minorities, the less marginalized they will be."

-Sean Baker

CONCEPTUAL COMPONENT SUMMARIES

1. ***Who Am I?*** — The key to being an effective leader is to have a true understanding of who you are as an individual and the roles that you play in your life circles. Participants begin to make the connections between their individual identities and the roles they play in their lives.

2. ***Critical Thinking*** — In order to develop a true understanding and application of the key components and characteristics of transformational leadership, participants explore the ways that they process and learn information in a variety of situations to develop a fundamental understanding of the ways in which they process information to make decisions as transformational leaders.

Through an examination of Gardner's theory of Multiple Intelligences and Johari's Windows, participants have the opportunity to create their own strategic learning plan as the precursor to developing strategic plans for groups/teams that they may be leading through their roles as transformational leaders.

3. ***Team Building*** — A hallmark of transformational leaders is their ability to bring together individuals within a group to work together, collaborate effectively and ultimately grow into becoming leaders themselves—taking direct responsibility for the outcomes of their actions. Participants examine the dynamics of group interaction and the importance of team building in the transformational leadership process.

4. ***Cultural Diversity*** — A good transformational leader must consider the backgrounds and cultural footprints of their team in order to make sound decisions. As part of the unit, participants explore the effect that cultural norms, beliefs, and ways of thinking affect group dynamics and impact leadership decisions across a variety of situations.

5. ***Real World Events*** — Participants examine real world events and critically assess the role of leaders in each situation. This examination of real-world application of leadership theory allows participants to further develop their understanding of the concepts presented.

6. ***Leadership Attributes*** — Participants examine the actions of leaders and have an opportunity to speak to community leaders to further develop their concept of the characteristics and roles of transformational leaders.

7. ***Communication*** — Participants examine the various ways in which messages are communicated—both verbal and nonverbal and assesses their ability to communicate and interact effectively with various groups. The importance and role of communication in leadership is explored and participants have the opportunity to develop their own theories and strategies to improve communication within a group.

8. ***Being Transformational*** — This component provides participants with a way of putting the theory of Johari's Windows into practice and identify various ways in which they can be transformational leaders in their communities.

9. ***Who Am I*** — This component provides participants with an opportunity to express who they are as transformational leaders, after have gone through each of the core pillars through this transformational leadership model.

You can surmise from the conceptual summaries of the core pillars that numbers 1 & 9 are both the same. That is not by mistake but rather by divine intervention because, along the way, the participants' behavior changes for the good, and a 360-degree transformation takes place.

Individuals begin the transformational leadership process but exit the process as new creatures of habit and have experienced 360 Degrees of Evolution. The 360-Degrees of Evolution occurs when and only when individuals are honest with themselves by identifying their strengths and weaknesses and remain optimistic about changing from stage one of the leadership model.

The nine core pillars of these transformational leadership models are not meant to be a means to an end but a stepping-stone or a continuation of self-exploration with a focus on leadership that leads to positive change and outcomes in one's life. Any core pillars can be made interchangeable with other pillars, models, or programs to add a more substantial value to the objective and goal.

Now let's dive deeper into the nine core pillars chosen for these transformational leadership models and further understand why they are so significant in developing you as a leader.

WHAT'S THE RELATIONSHIP BETWEEN DTD'S TRANSFORMATIONAL LEADERSHIP MODELS AND LEADERSHIP DEVELOPMENT?

Are leaders born or made? This discussion has been one that goes as far back as pre-historic dinosaurs, and depending on who you ask, can be answered one way or another. In my professional experience, leaders can be made and from my personal beliefs, leaders can be born.

From my personal beliefs, everyone is born with a soul, which is in essence connected to the Holy Spirit. Through the guidance and facilitation from the Holy Spirit, individuals learn to know what is right and what is wrong in life. Individuals learn to know what is right and what is wrong through their parents, environment, culture, surroundings, role models, and society.

Those that are trusted to lead and guide these individuals are also filled with the Holy Spirit. When individuals are connected and remain connected with the higher being he/she believes in and stay connected with that higher being, then transformation begins from the inside out versus the outside in, that remains evident in their behaviors, actions, communications, choices made and the way people are impacted (Positive versus Negative, Selfish gain versus Selfless gain, Transformational versus Transactional).

Dr. Tekemia Dorsey's (DTD) Transformational Leadership Models Through the personal growth and development from a two-step process, leaders are born and not made. The two-step process encompasses the guidance and facilitation led by the Holy Spirit and executed by individuals. All that is really needed in life is that of belief and execution of what we really are and that is a spiritual being living in a borrowed body which is known as the "flesh" therefore the POWER we need to be Leaders already exist inside each and every one, It simply needs to be tapped into needs to simply be tapped into, but if it were that simple, the author would not have developed DTD's Transformational Leadership Models or feel the need to write this book.

True Leadership Lies In the POWER of the HOLY SPIRIT
™ Dr. Tekemia Dorsey

From my professional experience, leaders can be made. Leaders are made through the quality of leadership development and training models and programs. Ones that can provide tangible outcomes and realistic tools for success. Leadership development models, training, and programs that an individual can use and improve upon, not just Dr. Tekemia Dorsey's (DTD) Transformational Leadership Models those that are filled with fluff. Leadership development models, trainings, and programs that infuse research, theory, and practical application; one that has been validated and has a solid foundation that is applicable across one's growth and development stages; one or two such as Dr. Tekemia Dorsey's (DTD) Transformational Leadership Models.

BRIEF HISTORY - DTD'S TRANSFORMATIONAL LEADERSHIP MODELS

Dr. Tekemia Dorsey's (DTD) Transformational Leadership Models (Secular VS Spiritual) which was created in 2006 but were originally leadership development, training, and education models (Secular and Spiritual). Dr. Tekemia Dorsey's Transformational Leadership Models evolved from extensive research and semi-structure and structural interviews with over 100 educators, leaders, supervisors, parents, and teachers from 2004 - 2007.

DTD's Transformational Leadership Models were originally Leadership Development Training and Education Models that were piloted to elementary and middle school aged youth in Private Christian school settings from 2007 - 2010. In 2010, the secular leadership development, training and education model/curriculum was adopted by a public school system in Baltimore City that served at-risk youth. The curriculum was enhanced from its previous version to meet the needs of young adults' ages 16 to 21 years young.

Once the population expanded to a new targeted audience served (business owners, entrepreneurs, corporations, workforce development centers, etc), DTD's Transformational Leadership Model dropped its education component to focus more on the core pillars of the transformational leadership models.

Models are designed to take ordinary people and transform them to extraordinary leaders through 360 degrees of evolution through a focus on nine core pillars.

> "When you use the term minority or minorities in reference to people, you're telling them that they're less than somebody else."
>
> **-Gwendolyn Brooks**

DR. TEKEMIA DORSEY'S (DTD) TRANSFORMATIONAL LEADERSHIP MODELS

The core pillars of DTD's Transformational Leadership Model are discussed in this book individually. Each one is an independent pillar of its own but are also dependent on one another for success as a leader. Through stories and real-life scenarios, the model itself are shared in practical application in how they work together to have ordinary people transformed into extraordinary leaders by experiencing the 360 Degrees of Evolution.

The DTD's Transformational Leadership Models are universal across industries and disciplines respectively and is applicable to individuals from individuals such as youth, to CEOs of Corporation.

This book should be used interchangeably in academic settings and business cultures and environments. The contents of this book can be used as part of curriculum for youth in primary grades and on secondary levels, for those individuals going through workforce development programs, for students who are pursuing advanced degrees, for individuals looking to start a business, enhance their business, or to climb that ladder of success in positions within their corporate settings.

The DTD's Transformational Leadership Models core pillars are ones that focus on personal growth and development of a person and their behaviors. The content of the book can be used as part of any structural program, training or activity that focuses on improvement of Dr. Tekemia Dorsey's (DTD) Transformational Leadership Models self, soft skills development and as such but not limited to professional development, leadership training, personal growth, and development.

Definition of Terms

1. Who Am I - finding out and exploring one's purpose and passion in life.

2. Critical Thinking - disciplined thinking that is clear, rational, open-minded, and informed by evidence.

3. Team Building - the use of different types of team interventions that are aimed at enhancing social relations and clarifying team members' roles as well as solving task and interpersonal problems that affect team functioning.

4. Cultural Diversity - is the acceptance of the various ethnic cultures in schools, organizations, businesses, neighborhoods, or cities. At the best, it involves treating impartially and fairly each ethnic group without promoting the particular beliefs or values of any group.

5. Real World Events - events of the world that occur daily in and around society.

6. Leadership Attributes - defined as characteristics, behaviors, and actions of the individual that help in the identification of the person.

7. Communication - is defined as ways or processes of expressing feelings or ideas which can be through verbal and nonverbal mean, expressions, body language, and so forth.

8. Be Transformational - the manner in which a person carries him/herself in the company of another, allowing their presence to impact positively on the environment or setting.

9. 360 Degrees of Evolution – Who Am I? – a metamorphosis takes place through behavioral change throughout the process

Dr. Tekemia Dorsey's (DTD) Transformational Leadership Models 360 Degrees of Evolution

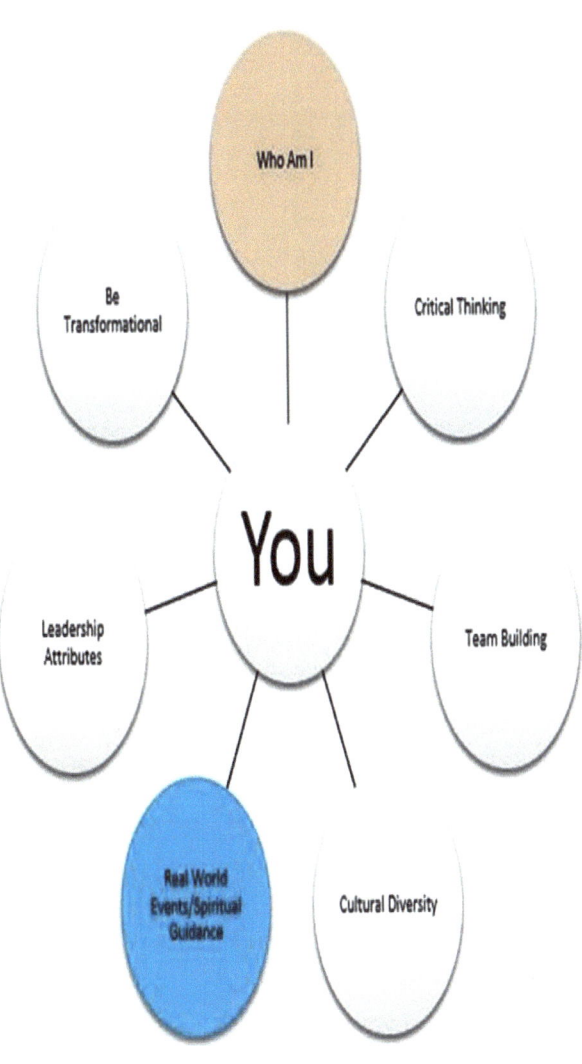

> "I think the biggest problem of the 21st century is how to deal with minorities."
>
> -Avigdor Lieberman

CORE PILLAR 1: WHO AM I?

It will take the span of one's life to truly understand the question WHO AM I? What makes this exciting is the fact that each day a person has breath, he/she has an opportunity to learn something new about "self" and to make a difference with that newfound knowledge. On the contrary, what makes the exploration of self, less attractive is the facing of the untruth a person has held onto as a value and reality for so long. However, even the ugliest of ugly situations can be changed if one truly wants change and transformation to occur.

The Struggle

It is a daily struggle for people to truly know, accept, and embrace who they are as an individual and in the multitude of roles they are involved in and their responsibilities on a daily basis. Women, who are in corporate positions, are wives, with children and other social responsibilities coupled with struggles they faced on a daily basis in their various communities.

Due to the nature of women to want to help and nurture others, they often overlook on many occasions their own needs and wants for that of others.

When women allow the needs of others to supersede their own, their worlds tend to be upside down. Instead of the woman being on top and the world being her portal of endless opportunity for success, the world sits on the top and the woman at the bottom unsure of how to turn things around in her life.

Picture 1

Picture 2

Picture 3

a. Mental

The #1 struggle for women, like all individuals whose world is turned upside down is that of their mental state. When a woman's mind is not at peace, not clear, not at ease and constantly racing then everything else in her life will be experiencing the same and it will affect decisions made, relationships engaged in, and negative behaviors such as fear, anxiety, procrastination, uncertainty, and low self-esteem continue to be a normal part of their daily behavior and routine. Poor decision making, unhealthy relationships, and the behaviors described above prohibit them from making positive attributes to them and everyone around them. If you ask a woman how she would break this cycle of trauma she is inflicting on herself and those directly and those around her, she would not be sure, but would want to believe her situation as not real.

b. Physical Struggle.

When a woman's state of mind is disconnected from her realities, another area of concern becomes their physical state. Women are emotional creatures and when they start to experience emotional or physical stress, they revert to food. The same goes true to cultural barriers that exist such as with African Americans and Hispanics, these cultures are known for their eating habits.

These does not mean all African Americans and Hispanics are over eaters. Some, maybe most women either eat their way through stress or workout stress related issues. Very few falls in the latter category but quite a few in the former category. When women experience fear, anxiety, uncertainty, procrastination, self-confidence, and even stress what is one of the most common behaviors exhibited to combat the disorder of their minds, their lives, and their situation? They eat. Things such as chips, soda, candy, junk food, fried foods, massive sugar, and other unhealthy choices become the cure for the current problem which leads to an obese body and depression.

b. Spiritual Struggle.

Women are naturally spiritual creatures that believe in a power higher than self. World situations and the roles women take on such as a mother, wife, or even corporate executive are often time ones that do not allow too much time for self, unless it is on Sunday. Most women on Sundays simply want to rest and do nothing after a very busy week. Their spiritual connection which is balance for most women are then being sacrificed even more than usual.

When a woman's mental, physical, and spiritual balances are not equal, then they will lack the peace of mind and a sense of self for success, often leaving them asking themselves, WHO AM I?

The question "WHO AM I" is an evolutionary concept that can take a lifetime to master however, the more one begins to examine who they are and what they stand for, how one handles the challenges of life makes all the difference. In the Dr. Tekemia Dorsey's (DTD) Transformational Leadership Model, many tools and assessments are used but one of my favorites remains that of Johari's Window.

The Johari window test was named after the first names of its inventors: Joseph Luft and Harry Ingham, "Of Human Interaction" (Mayfield Publishing Co., Palo Alto, CA: 1969).

The Johari window - which represents self - looks like this:

Johari's Windows

Before

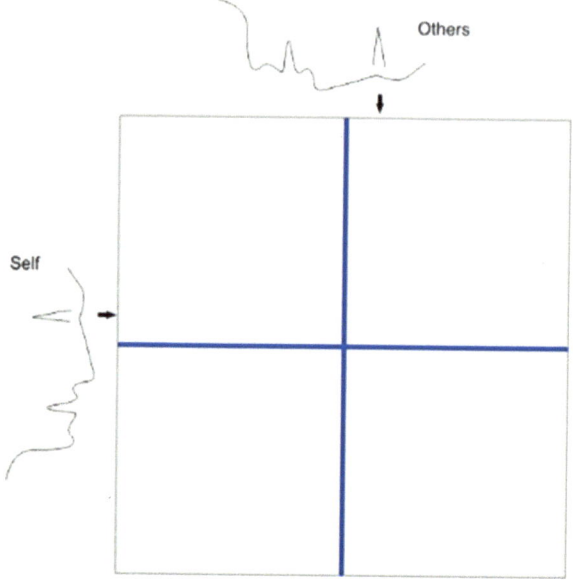

After

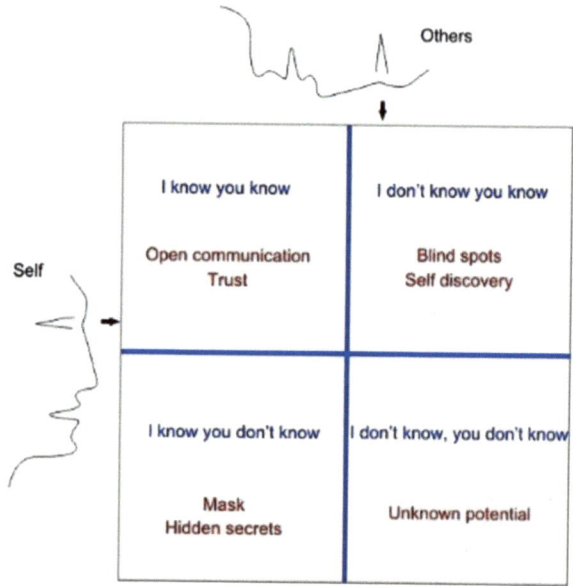

Johari's Window is a tool used to help individuals become even more aware of self and to reaffirm self. This is a wonderful tool as a part of DTD's Transformational Leadership Model to assist people going from ordinary to extraordinary leaders.

The author believes self-awareness is one of the greatest gifts we have in our toolbox for success.

In the Dr. Tekemia Dorsey's (DTD) Transformational Leadership Model, the key to being an effective leader is to have a true understanding of who you are as an individual and the roles that you play in your life circles. Participants begin to make the connections between their individual identities and the roles they play in their lives during the exploration of the core pillar, WHO AM I?

WHO AM I? – YOUTH PERSPECTIVE
How does this apply from an urban youth perspective?

"Life is now a war zone, and as such, the number of people considered disposable has grown exponentially, and this includes low-income whites, poor minorities, immigrants, the unemployed, the homeless, and a range of people who are viewed as a liability to capital and its endless predatory quest for power and profits."

-Henry Giroux

CORE PILLAR 2: CRITICAL THINKING

Humans by nature keep their hands in more than their fair share of the cookie jar. When this happens, they are left overwhelmed, unsure, and scatter-brained to say the least. Instead of them being able to provide a roadmap to success for self, they tend to go into any direction that leaves them frustrated, upset, bewildered, anxious, and panicky.

Women who wear many hats such as wife, mother, community leader, community organizer, community volunteer, or even corporate executive has their fair share of days where everything and everyone one has a lot in common.

For a corporate executive, responsibilities such as administrative, decision making, personnel, meetings on various levels, trainings, conferences, workshops, and a few other things during the course of the day are just a few things needing attention.

Then, if that corporate executive is a mom, she now has Mommy duties which requires attention just as those given at work including homework, teacher conferences, follow ups, concerns and let's not consider if it is more than one child she has.

A woman's daily schedule with her family for the day could very much reflect the following:

Semi Aggressive Family Schedule

6:00 AM - Wake Up - Mommy
6:30 AM - Family Dress, Breakfast
7:00 AM - Drop off to Daycare/School 7:15 AM - Off to work
8:30 AM - Arrive to work
5:00 PM - Leave from work
6:30 PM - Pick up family from Aftercare 7:00 PM - Arrive Home
7:30 PM - Eat Dinner
8:00 PM - Check homework
9:30 PM - Prayer/Bedtime for Family 9:45 PM - Mommy off to bed

Now this potential scheduling which is very reflective of an average family with kids is truly aggressive but what is missing is the activity which most kids today are involved in.

Where in the course of the day does the mother have to herself; to think act or engage self or life? What impact can a schedule like this have on the mind, body, spirit, and soul after a while?

Now let us examine the same family dynamics with activities built in:

Aggressive Family Schedule

6:00 AM - Wake Up - Mommy
6:30 AM - Family Dress, Breakfast
7:00 AM - Drop off to Daycare/School 7:15 AM - Off to work
8:30 AM - Arrive to work
4:00 PM - Leave work early
5:30 PM - Pick up family from Aftercare
6:00 PM - Sports Activities (Practice/Games) 8:30 PM - Pick up dinner from fast food place 9:00 PM - Arrive Home
9:15 PM - Eat Dinner
9:45 PM - Check homework 10:45 PM - Bath
11:15 PM - Prayer/Bedtime for Family 12:00 AM - Mommy off to bed

This schedule in conjunction with the schedule above (Semi Aggressive Family Schedule) are realistic today for parents with active kids. What happens is burn out, exhaustion, poor body image, unhealthy decision making, irritability, low self-esteem, lack of intimacy and most importantly, and a loss of self.

In the Dr. Tekemia Dorsey's (DTD) Transformational Leadership Models, a multitude of assessments and tools are used for success but one of the author's favorites is that of Howard Gardener's Multiple Intelligences. Through the use of this tool, one's talents are discovered and applied for success.

Below are Howard Gardner's Multiple Intelligences Theory and a simple grid diagram that illustrates his seven multiple intelligences model at a glance.

Howard Gardner's Multiple Intelligence Simple Grid

intelligence type	capability and perception
Linguistic	words and language
Mathematical	logic and numbers
Musical	music, sound, rhythm
Bodily-Kinesthetic	body movement control
Spatial-Visual	images and space
Interpersonal	other people's feelings
Intrapersonal	self-awareness

A mother with aggressive schedules such as above would learn their "intelligence language" drive deeper into its understanding and begin to make changes that allow a more balance sense of self however without learning about ones "intelligence language" and thinking critically through the situation presented, failure remains imminent.

In order to develop a true understanding and application of the key components and characteristics of transformational leadership, participants explore the various ways in which information is acquired in varieties of situations and ability to make decisions as transformational leaders. Through an examination of Gardner's theory of Multiple Intelligences and Johari's Windows, participants have the opportunity to create their own strategic learning plan as the precursor to developing strategic plans for real application in situations that they may be find themselves through their roles as transformational leaders, such as their families in this core pillar, Critical Thinking.

CRITICAL THINKING – YOUTH PERSPECTIVE
How does this apply to an urban youth perspective?

"I would argue that we have a generation of young people, particularly minorities, who are no longer putting up with the kinds of things their parents put up with. They're much more self-confident. It's no longer acceptable to make fun of people because of race or sex. But it has always been present in American society."

-Donna Shalala

CORE PILLAR 3: TEAM BUILDING

A woman with a family and active kids with Semi or Aggressive Family Schedules as discussed before and shared below, is displaying an "I" in a team because everything as it appears, is done by that one person. While the schedule provided, is one very reflective of families in America today, one or two elements could be added or removed but nevertheless, one person attempting to do it all is far from realistic.

Semi Aggressive Family Schedule

6:00 AM - Wake Up - Mommy
6:30 AM - Family Dress, Breakfast
7:00 AM - Drop off to Daycare/School 7:15 AM - Off to work
8:30 AM - Arrive to work
5:00 PM - Leave from work
6:30 PM - Pick up family from Aftercare 7:00 PM - Arrive Home
7:30 PM - Eat Dinner
8:00 PM - Check homework
9:30 PM - Prayer/Bedtime for Family 9:45 PM - Mommy off to bed

With this semi aggressive family schedule, it is possible that one person could handle, has handled and will continue to handle it. However, at what costs? Is it at the expense of their sanity, mental state, physical appearance, energy level, relationships gained or lost, burn out and being overwhelmed?

Aggressive Family Schedule

6:00 AM - Wake Up - Mommy
6:30 AM - Family Dress, Breakfast
7:00 AM - Drop off to Daycare/School 7:15 AM - Off to work
8:30 AM - Arrive to work
4:00 PM - Leave work early
5:30 PM - Pick up family from Aftercare
6:00 PM - Sports Activities (Practice/Games) 8:30 PM - Pick up dinner from fast food place 9:00 PM - Arrive Home
9:15 PM - Eat Dinner
9:45 PM - Check homework 10:45 PM - Bath
11:15 PM - Prayer/Bedtime for Family 12:00 AM - Mommy off to bed

With this aggressive family schedule, it is possible that one person could handle it, has handled, and will continue to handle it; however, the likelihood of success over time is far greater than that of the semi aggressive family schedule. Here's why? The focus is more about the outcome than the process and leaves one to experience mental and physical breakdowns and at what costs? Is it that of their lack of sanity, mental state, physical appearance, energy level, relationships gained or lost, burn out and being overwhelmed, early death, aneurysms developed disassociation with reality?

It Takes a Village

The bible says it takes a village to raise a child; this metaphor can be adapted to any situation or scenario. In this case, it is one of a woman with a family and active kids that should not attempt to do things on her own that requires 24/7 care and implementation. In this situation what resources will this woman need to explore in term of opportunities; resources, and people who can assist her with one of more of the events in her schedule that will provide less of a wear and tear on her? How can she leverage to her support network to create a win-win scenario for her and her family? The key remains within self (no more, no less).

Women are individuals that believe they can do it all and can take on the world. Women believe that, depending on their cultural beliefs and family upbringing, they should try things themselves first and ask for help later. In essence there is nothing wrong with being responsible for what they desire to want out of life, but when does one realize when things become too much?

In essence there is nothing wrong with being responsible for what they desire to want out of life, but when does one realize when things become too much?

The benefits of openly communicating the need for help or assistance does not include one of being a loser or sell out. The benefits of seeking balance in life does not allude to the fact, one will be viewed as weak but in all honesty strong by those that matters most, the family and the kids.

There has been an emphasis during this pillar of teamwork on the individual mainly because while there is no "I" in team, before there is a team, a bunch of "I's" need to come to the table knowing his/her strengths and areas of challenges for an overall balance for success as part of a team and in the building of a team.

In this example, the more the woman know of herself (strengths and weaknesses) and things she need help with (an extra person for driving, support, etc), the more probable success factor in building a team will occur. On the contrary, if a woman in this scenario fails to identify her strengths and weaknesses (who am I), think critically accessing her situation to determine success (critical thinking), and to begin to reach across parties lines for assistance (teamwork), she is destined to be less transformational in nature and more transactional, which benefits no one.

"A hallmark of transformational leaders is their ability to bring together individuals within a group to work together, collaborate effectively and ultimately grow into becoming leaders themselves—taking direct responsibility for outcomes of their actions. Participants examine the dynamics of group interaction and the importance of team building in the transformational leadership process"

Dr. Tekemia Dorsey

TEAM BUILDING – YOUTH PERSPECTIVE
How does this apply to an urban youth perspective?

> "The most certain test by which we judge whether a country is really free is the amount of security enjoyed by minorities."
>
> -John Dalberg-Acton

CORE PILLAR 4: CULTURAL DIVERSITY

The world is made up of diverse cultures but these concepts, individually and collectively are often not valued or identified as important. The world is made up of different people, with different backgrounds, similarities and differences but are not often accepted. This is a huge concern.

The similarities and differences in each of us is what makes us unique and odd, but people are not really able to see, understand, and accept the differences of others. People say they do in theory but does not so much in application. Look at the scenarios regarding Michael Brown and Trayvon Martin, celebrities such as Kim Kardashian West and Kanye West, the public defamation and disrespect of our President, Barack Obama and First Lady Michelle Obama, just to name a few.

In the scenario with the active family woman, society would automatically place her in a category of "single and poor class" because a mate or husband has not been added to the script, how wrong could that assumption be? A person's bias and prejudice based on his/her upbringing, own culture and environment, foundational principles such as beliefs, morals, and values are those that add to the struggle of diversity in cultures or contribute positively to the charge because an individual is able to view another for who and what he/she is.

The former is what happens 99.9% of the time, and the former less than .1%. The world is made up of a melting pot of cultures, races, ethnicities, various likes and dislikes, similarities and differences, beliefs, morals and values and each person are fearfully and wonderfully made in HIS (God's) image. It would be a powerful thing if we could respect one another for who and what we are, the world would be a better place. However, in order for that to occur, the world would need to start all over again from scratch and be rid of the imperfection inherited over centuries that extend back to our ancestors.

When people are not able to value one another, then it makes it difficult for true partnerships and relationships to be formed. When a woman has experienced bad relationships, hurt, a lack of trust, pain, heartache, and distress because of a person, especially one of statue or significance such as a leader, then that emotion or experience is now defined by that person. When a woman who needs assistance or seek help with a concern is forced to work with or settle for a person representative of a past mistake, then the outcome is not positive. As a result of that barrier, teamwork needed is not achieved. What will it take for a person to accept another person for what they represent?

In the Dr. Tekemia Dorsey's (DTD) Transformational Leadership Model, cultural diversity is thoroughly discussed, because understanding a person for who and what he/she is and represents is needed for short term and long-term success. Most are not quick to trust another which bring a variety of concerns to the table (scenarios). The more educated a person is the more time he/she will take to explore others who are not well educated as he is through their ethnicity, culture, socioeconomic environment, religious affiliation, personal bias and prejudice, sexual orientation, political affiliation, and social cues.

"A good transformational leader must consider the backgrounds and cultural footprints of their team in order to make sound decisions. As a part of the unit, participants explore the effect of cultural norms, beliefs and ways of thinking affect group dynamics and impact leadership decisions across a variety of situations"

Dr. Tekemia Dorsey

CULTURAL DIVERSITY – YOUTH PERSPECTIVE
How does this apply to an urban youth perspective?

CORE PILLAR 5: REAL WORLD EVENTS/SPIRITUAL GUIDANCE

People look at the world through different lens and the set of lenses that appear the most real to them are those that their reality is based off. The two sets of lenses referred here are real world events or spiritual events.

Real World Events

Most people are motivated by the events of the world. Those events can either remind them of what reality truly is to keep them going or it serves as a life reminder and sends them into a deeper depression or feeling depressed. Real world events such as the birth of a baby, an extension of the family through marriage, a promotion at work, an increase in pay, kids achieving good grades, individuals accomplishing personal goals, or a combination of any of the above are examples of what keeps people filled with hope, faith, and setting new goals and achieving them. Real world events bring joy, happiness, excitement, a sense of empowerment and self-gratification to people. People remain inspired to what the world has to offer but then there is the other side that people must deal with in their reality that is not so positive or happy-happy-joy-joy either.

Real world events present heartache, pain, grief, setback, trials, and tribulations, death, despair loss of a job, uncertainty, fear, and depression that cause a low sense of self, a disconnect between fantasy and reality for some, and oftentimes, forcing people to say things, do things and act in a manner that is unbecoming to their character and family values.

Real world events can either uplift or challenge one's state of mind.

Real world events even if caused by a setback requires a strong comeback. One that is positive in nature and requires productivity of life. However, for that to happen people must think critically through the situation, reach across the party lines to build their team of support and resources, understand the cultural diversity embodied in the scenario, but most importantly know who they are entering this journey, check self along the way, and evaluate their growth once it is over.

Real world events such as life struggles and challenges are meant for people to grow mind, body, soul, and spirit in every facet, role, responsibility, hat worn, relationships entered and exited along the way. For every situation we go through, we should come out of the other side of it, a new creature whether it be mind, body, soul, spirit, or a combination of one or more of the above.

Real world events such as life struggles and challenges can be presented to people in different ways and impacting various stages of one's life. However, it is now what is presented to you in know that matters, but it is, how you handle it. Women, for example as discussed earlier take on many roles, massive responsibilities, and usually overwhelmed themselves all in the matter of a day, week or month, with or without active children, a husband or extended family to care for.

Real world events such as becoming a mom for the first time, getting married, caring for an elderly parent, having a 2nd or 3rd child, being an active member in the community, serving as Team Mom of a child's organization event (sports, nonprofit organization), and even mentoring others are real things for women that cannot be altered or face anyway other than head on. Most women embrace, accept, and openly accept the journeys presented to them but not all women.

Some women do not want to be a mother or think they feel they want in the beginning to then realize; motherhood is not what they thought it would be or can now handle. Some women like the thought of being married, a wife, someone's partner only to find out that marriage is like a job, but it takes time to learn what marriage is truly, to develop a formula for success, and to understand there is a HUGE difference between being single and being married. Once realized what is required to be married, in a marriage and to remain in a marriage, some women no longer remain interested in being marries.

Some women want to be viewed as philanthropic and are moved by the thought of volunteer work but it like marriage, being a wife, and having kids, too is work. It requires time, patience, good decision making, great communication, and the ability to know what she is already bringing to the table in terms of strengths and areas of improvement.

When starting any new journey, new venture, new goals set, if a person truly embrace the strengths and areas of improvement within self, from the old, a new creature is born. When a person starts their day, from sun-up when a person rises, to sundown (when a person rests), a transformation from the old to the new should occur because when a person gains knowledge and applies it in terms of wisdom in each interaction, decision made, scenario presented and end result, a different person emerge. No every person understands or desire to know the transformation that happens on a daily basis but when they do, the probability of positive growth, development, and outcome in one's life remains endless.

When real world events become too much to bear, some people balance the reality of what is real with that of something higher in which they believe in, for the sake of this discussion, it is being identified as Spiritual Guidance. Real world events can either make or break the development of leaders however I believe that everyone is automatically born because of the Holy Spirit that dwells within.

Spiritual Guidance

Some people are motivated by the guidance of the Holy Spirit that lives within them. Instead of turning to the events of the world they intuitively listened to what the Holy Spirit says to them and encourages them to do in terms of movement, relationships, behaviors, etc. Just like the events of the world, a person experience heartaches and pains, trials and tribulations, successes and failures however in addition to, or in opposition of real-world events, people lean on the faith and comfort that the word of God to get them through tough times and cause for additional celebration during good times.

The guidance of one's faith and belief in a power higher than self is largely dependent of the individual and cannot be refuted in terms of impacts in one's life and affect in their behaviors and actions. However, who their higher power is whether its God, Allah, etc can be a topic of discussion.

In the application and training of Dr. Tekemia Dorsey's (DTD) Transformational Leadership Models, these two core pillars are what makes the difference in the models. One model is one of the secular nature (real world events) where real world events are used as part of the teachings and applications and whereas the other (spiritual guidance) is one of spiritual reflection and the principles enforced by the teachings of the bible are used in terms of delivery, re-enforcement and practical application of the training.

Whether it is real world events or spiritual guidance that motivates and guides a person through the journey he/she undergoes, the same remains are that there is or should be a transformation of the old to the new once the end result is reached, when a person allows growth to happen.

REAL WORLD EVENTS – YOUTH PERSPECTIVE
How does this apply to an urban youth perspective?

"The big problem is that a lot of Americans, whether they are underrepresented minorities or from rural areas, do not know about career opportunities in the tech industry because they may not have had role models who are part of this field or learned about STEM in school."

-Stacy Brown-Philpot

CORE PILLAR 6: LEADERSHIP ATTRIBUTES

Are leaders born or made? This discussion has been one that goes as far back as pre-historic dinosaurs and, depending on who you ask, can be answered one way or another. In my professional experience, leaders can be made, and from my personal beliefs, leaders can be born. Everyone is born with a soul connected to the Holy Spirit, from my personal beliefs. Through the guidance and facilitation of the Holy Spirit, individuals learn to know what is right and what is wrong in life. Individuals learn to know what is right and what is through their parents, environment, culture, surroundings, role models, and society.

Those trusted to lead and guide these individuals are also filled with the Holy Spirit. When individuals connect with their higher being, transformation begins from the inside out versus the opposite. Transformation takes shape through behaviors, actions, communications, decisions, and how people are impacted.

Through the personal growth and development from a two-step process, leaders are born and not made. The two-step process encompasses the guidance and facilitation led by the Holy Spirit and Dr. Tekemia Dorsey's (DTD) Transformational Leadership Models executed by individuals. All that is needed in life is that belief and execution of what we are: a spiritual being living in a borrowed body known as the "flesh." The POWER needed to be leaders already lives inside each of us. The power needs to be unleashed from within.

"True Leadership Lies In the POWER of the HOLY SPIRIT"
Dr. Tekemia Dorsey

Through the training from Dr. Tekemia Dorsey's (DTD) Transformational Leadership Models, participants examine the actions of leaders. They have an opportunity to speak to community leaders to develop further their concept of the characteristics and roles of transformational leaders. Additionally, participants explore, unveil, and accept the leadership attributes within each and apply those attributes to their lives. Participants develop a plan of action for their lives that allows personal growth and development of their plans and desires (i.e., family, community, work, relationships, career, etc.).

Youth Leaders-In-Training (2015)

Dr. Dorsey's oldest son, Brandon, now 17 years old, was a part of the original pilot study of students who engaged in and completed her leadership development, training, and education certificate program. Dorsey used the spiritual leadership version of her transformational leadership model. At the time, Brandon was attending a private Christian school in Baltimore County, MD, where he was just in 3rd grade. From 3rd - to 8th grades, Brandon engaged in the transformational leadership program, graduating from the program several times year after year.

Brandon has held and continues to hold leadership positions such as:

- Middle River Parks and Recreation Youth Football Coach Intern 2 Years
- Hair Doctors Barbershop Intern - 8 years
- Annual Adopt A Family Christmas Program - 11 years
- National Literacy Mentorship Program - 5 years
- Cristo Rey High School Intern - 3 years
- Top Teens of America Vice President - 2 Years

In his final year of high school, Brandon gave several speeches at a recent induction of youth for the Top Teens of America Spring Induction Ceremony. His theme choice was reflective of his views and training endured over the years, which had made him into the fine young scholar and leader he was that day.

Dr. Dorsey developed the leadership development, training, and educational curriculum and program initiatives to see if the concept of leadership could be taught to a targeted population younger than 9th grade.

In Fall 2007, Dr. Tekemia Dorsey's (DTD) Transformational Leadership program's initial launch was at a local private school. The private school housed students in K - 8th grade in one classroom. It was the first time Dorsey had been introduced to this school model. Dorsey was reluctant to implement the program with a gap in age disparities, grade differences, and maturity levels amongst the targeted population. For over a decade, Dorsey's background as a school counselor professional and educator had not seen or been introduced to the integration of such diversity in students in a cohort setting. Based on widespread research at the time (2007), the success of such diversity in a cohort of diverse students was not imminent. Several private school systems piloted the one schoolroom concept around the US to explore whether the concept was viable.

Supported programming was needed with the new concept of a one schoolroom model concept for private schools. Before 2007, leadership training and development programs were only implemented on the secondary levels (9th -12th grades). Leadership training and development was not a concept closely associated with elementary or middle-aged students.

Based on Dorsey's decade-long experience as a professional school counselor/educator and knowledge acquisition through research and doctoral studies, Dr. Dorsey set out to explore if leadership training and development could be taught to elementary and middle school-aged youth.

While Dorsey explored if leadership training and development could be taught, the K-8 participants from the one schoolroom model classroom demonstrated leadership training and development could be taught to a targeted audience younger than 9th grade. K-8 participants engaged in and completed a year-long leadership training and development program and were the first graduate cohort of Dr. Tekemia Dorsey's Leadership 2 Transform Leaders.

Within the first 5-7 years of a program, if youth are taught core pillars of leadership training centered on their personal growth and development, their future and our society and community remain more than hopeful and prosperous. Also, as adults, they will continue to impact lives positively.

Brandon C. Johnson,
Kenwood High School Senior
Age 17
Delivering GREAT LEADERS Speech
Top Teens of America Induction Ceremony
Spring, 2015

Empowering TRIathletes To LEAD

YOUTH IN LEADERSHIP TRAINING (2020 & 2021)

How does this apply to youth from an urban perspective?
Check out Case Studies

Great Leaders...

Awaken minds.
Bring people together.
Communicate effectively. Dare to take calculated risks.
Enlighten and empower.
Foster collaboration.
Give you tools to succeed.
Help you do for yourself. Invite and encourage questions.
Joyfully embrace diversity.

Keep an open mind.
Lead by example.
Motivate with respect.
Never give up on you.
Open doors to new worlds.
Put first things first.
Quest to make learning fun.
Recognize problems early.
Share roles and responsibilities.

Take time to explain things.
Unwrap talents and abilities.
Value everyone's input.
Welcome mistakes as part of learning.

Xceed expectations.
Yearn to connect, not correct.
Zest to make a difference.

© Meiji Stewart.
www.ABCPoems.com

CORE PILLAR 7: COMMUNICATION

If not handled properly, communication can be a source of evil or the catalyst for a successful change. The sole reason why communication is essential is the various levels and ways we can connect. Communication is all about developing a connection with others, and when connections are made, relationships are built. When relationships are built and nourished, success remains imminent for all parties involved, regardless of the intellectual, number of degrees, socio-economic status, racial, ethnic, economic, or religious affiliation.

Individuals learn early on that it is not about what you say to people, but how you say it matters. It is possible to offend someone excellently by using the right words at the wrong time. Just the tone of your voice is enough to change the message you are passing across.

Our forefathers were forced to speak directly with one another face-to-face. With face-to-face communication, the message can still be misinterpreted by the messenger's tone, words, and body language. How those variables are received and interpreted by the receiver makes all the difference for relationships built and grow. As they say, the first impression makes a lasting impression.

Sender - Receive Message

Communication plays a significant role in how others perceive you. The primary language for communication is the English Language in the United States; however, when communicating with others, the primary English language can take on many levels when being interpreted depending on their background, culture, socioeconomic status, environment, or even ethnic affiliation. For example, the most common misinterpretation between African Americans and Caucasians is how the word "Negro" can be used and received.

Communication Barriers

For an African American to refer to another African American as a "Negra or Negro" is not deemed offensive; if a Caucasian referred to an African American as a Negro, then an offense will automatically be taken; why is that? This is the case because of ethnic and cultural barriers that go back centuries. Rightfully so, words used and the meaning of that word depending on who says it and who is in receipt of it makes a huge difference in successful or failed communication. Now that same word Negro in Spanish means Black, which denotes a color and does not reference race and cultural affiliations.

People communicate through language as well as dress and style choices. When most people see a person dressed in all black, regardless of race, culture, socioeconomic status, etc., it is typically associated with death and mourning of a loss; however, that is not always true, and it is often mistaken. People who are overweight and uncomfortable in their skin typically wear the color black because it makes them look slimmer, which makes them feel better about themselves. Teenagers can also view the color black as gothic, weird, and even depressed, which is not always accurate. The color of teenagers is often just an expression of who they are, such as the painting of their fingernails black and wearing the color choice black the majority of the time for various reasons.

Corporate women have been known to also use the color choice of Black as their choice of nail polish for the workplace for various reasons, such as the representation of colors of their favorite football team, an occasion of celebration, and so forth. Nevertheless, we understand here that communication portrayed through the sender's intent and how one receives it either helps in the success of communication or to the detriment of failure.

When dealing with face-to-face communication, how the sender relates a message and how the receiver receives the message will dramatically impact the success of relationships. In contrast, the face-to-face method continues to be the best method by which we communicate, and it still has levels that need to be considered and valued for success. We will explore that in the next book release and during training.

Times have changed drastically in terms of communication, mainly in part to Y2K at the turn of the 21st century, and ever since then, how we communicate has changed with the advent of the internet.

The Internet

The introduction of the Internet scared the majority of the world because it was so unknown however the launch of the Internet changed the way communication would forever be remembered as intimate, straightforward, clear cutting, and impactful.

The Internet took away the option of one's ability to communicate face-to-face. The Internet has created a situation whereby individuals are allowed to communicate without a natural face and for the receiver to interpret the message anyhow they feel. The Internet hindered rapport and the building of relationships. It opened up ways in which people could communicate secretly, causing relationships to be destroyed on the one hand and relationships being built on the other hand.

Once companies realized the power of the Internet in terms of efficiency, speed, and quantity versus quality, additional ways to communicate using the Internet's technology quickly evolved. From pagers to flip phones, to smartphones, to now watches, tablets, eyeglasses, earpieces, chips embedded in one's skin, etc. While all the advancement of technology through the Internet was deemed beneficial to society, businesses, and the stock markets, to name a few, it all remains the lack of effectively knowing how to communicate from a human-to-human point of view.

Individuals today, such as our youth, young adults, and individuals seeking to climb the ladder of influence and leadership positions, lack the proper training in the various ways in which to communicate with tiers of people within businesses, institutions of higher learning, as well as their very own peers. Unfortunately, a person cannot land a successful interview by sending a text message to Human Resources for consideration. An individual cannot send a text message or tag a person on Instagram as a follow-up to say "Thank You" for an interview. Communication should result in a "Win-Win" scenario for all parties involved, never one over the other.

Even with the most recent and often up-to-date technology, devices such as emoticons, it is still not an effective method of communication, and it devalues the relationships built and rapport between individuals. An individual in a job situation cannot communicate effectively using the "smiley face emoticon" with their supervisor, superior, or secretary. It simply lacks professionalism, and some people prefer not to use technology other than good ole fashion face-to-face communication.

In training from the Dr. Tekemia Dorsey's (DTD) Transformational Leadership Models, participants examine how messages are communicated—both verbal and nonverbal- and assess their effectiveness in communicating and interacting with various groups.

The importance and role of communication in leadership are explored, and participants have the opportunity to develop their theories and strategies to improve communication within a group.

COMMUNICATION – YOUTH PERSPECTIVE
How does this apply to youth from an urban perspective?

"Low-income people, racial or ethnic minorities, pregnant women, seniors, people with special needs, people in rural areas - they all have a much harder time accessing a dentist than other groups of Americans."

-Bernie Sanders

CORE PILLAR 8: BEING TRANSFORMATIONAL

Being transformational means the cause is more significant than any individual, and while that sounds great in theory, it is even more critical in execution. Individuals must put aside ego, bias, prejudice, negativity, past hurt, and even emotions that affect performance to create a positive environment that resonates well with others.

In any environment, individuals have the power to transform anything by simply being/herself. When a person walks into a room, people will automatically know whether that person is approachable or not. There is a saying that "First impressions last forever," and these impressions can either have a positive or not so positive ripple impact.

When people know who they are, what they can offer, their strengths and areas of improvement, and have a sense of balance and uncanny self-confidence, even on their bad days, they can either take the initiative to transform their societies or not. They can turn things upside down. They have the POWER within to change the atmosphere and culture in a room, an environment, and a person's mood by doing simple things right from the beginning.

When a person is presented with a situation of adversity, they should be able first to remember who they are (their strengths, areas of weaknesses), should immediately begin to think critically by unveiling the hidden cues for success, developing a plan of action that includes building a team, understanding the cultural diversity embodied in the situation, reflecting on what motivates a person to think outside the box, identifying the leadership attributes possessed and those of persons around them, ensuring effective communication and follow-up (being transformational versus transactional). Working in the best interest of everyone versus a select few.

In training with Dr. Tekemia Dorsey's (DTD) Transformational Leadership Models, participants explore Johari's Windows again but in a different manner that allows them to identify various ways to be agents of transformation in their communities and circles. The Johari window - which represents self - looks like this:

Johari's Windows

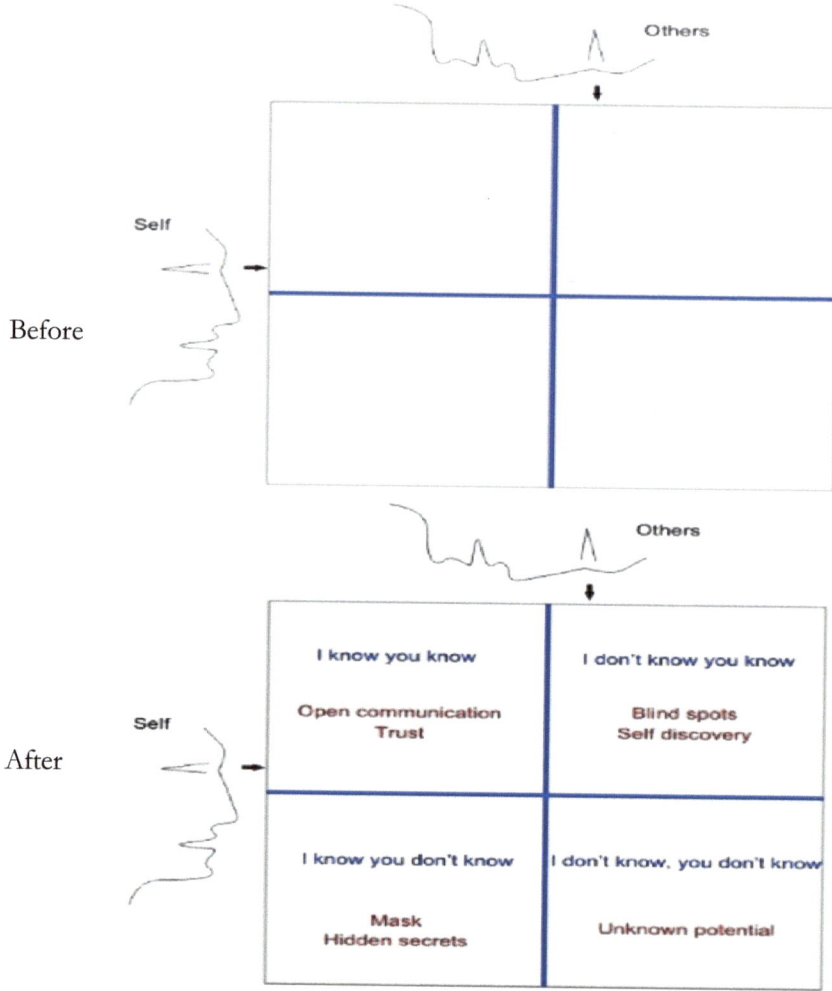

Johari's Window is a tool used to help individuals become even more aware of self and to reaffirm self. This is a wonderful tool as a part of DTD's Transformational Leadership Model to assist people going from ordinary to extraordinary leaders.

The author believes self-awareness is one of the greatest gifts we have in our toolbox for success.

360 DEGREE TRANSFORMATIONAL – YOUTH PERSPECTIVE
How does this apply to from an urban youth perspective?

CORE PILLAR 9: WHO AM I - 360 DEGREES OF EVOLUTION

A person that has evolved 360 degrees of evolution after going through each core pillar of this leadership model and have allowed growth to occur from the inside out. An individual goes from an ordinary individual to an extraordinary leader as they learn who they are and what they are truly capable of achieving. When applied to any scenario of life, due to a paradigm shift in thinking, outlook on life and self, participants are able to take the concepts learned and applied to any scenario in take, allowing for transformational leadership behaviors, actions, and outcomes.

Let's explore Dr.Tekemia Dorsey's(DTD) Transformational Leadership Models (360 Degrees of Evolution) applied to a scenario of someone wanting to become an entrepreneur.

Become an Entrepreneur

To move past a business owner mentality into an entrepreneurial mentality, you must first explore, recognize, and understand the concept of "Who AM I?" Understanding your strengths and weaknesses as a person and all the hats you wear in life, will help you determine how effective you will be as an individual, launching and continuing with your business successfully. Every business owner is not meant to be an entrepreneur.

To move past a business owner mentality to the entrepreneurial state-of-mind, you must critically think through the process by developing an action plan for success, such as who you are, what you want to accomplish, and what resources will be needed to make your dream a reality. Moving a plan from thought into manifestation takes time, energy, and careful consideration. Plan your work and work your plan.

To move past a business-owner mentality into an entrepreneurial mentality, you must not only believe there is no "I" in team, but you must begin implementing the concept through team building strategies. The challenge becomes not only exploring who you are but knowing what you can contribute to a team in terms of leadership, what you can learn from those in teams and how to balance the two in business.

To move past a business-owner mentality into an entrepreneurial state of mind, you must be able to identify and understand the cultural diversity of the world in business settings, business relationships, and the business culture of the organization. As an entrepreneur, you must understand the diversity that lies within each and every person you will come into contact with and never believe, think, or treat others as if they are all lump together under one category.

Knowing the uniqueness of culture and the impact that diversity has on business and within relationships will help your business go far. Each person on your team or part of your staff will bring similarities and differences to the table, but you as the leader will need to know how to balance the team successfully.

To move past a business-owner mentality into an entrepreneurial mentality, examine real world events that are occurring in life or seek spiritual guidance to ensure success. Events that happen in the world allow an entrepreneur that things will happen, but it is not what happens that define you however it is how you handle it that make all the difference. Seeking spiritual guidance from someone or something in life you believe in, provides clarity and understanding on how to act, approach, and address concerns of interests that may arise. Every day in life, you will encounter expected and sometimes unexpected challenges but as an entrepreneur you must find the power within to overcome the adversity presented.

To move past the business-owner mentality to the entrepreneurial state of mind, you must identify the leadership attributes that you already possess and the ones that have yet to be identified. Leadership attributes that already exists within you were discovered at some point along your life/upbringing, or through positive characteristics from you identify as role models in your life. Identifying your leadership attributes, what you stand for such as trust, loyalty, respect, honesty, stability, etc) will allow your business to progress in a manner that is satisfactory to you and that you can help grow along the way. As its company's leader, the organization will take on your characteristics, beliefs, morals, and values that are either good or not so good. If you are unsure about the leadership attributes you possess, seek assistance from a Life Coach or one that specializes in leadership growth and development.

To move past the business owner mentality into an entrepreneurial mentality, you must first explore, embrace and to learn to effectively execute the art of communication. Communication is a major factor that will decide if a business will succeed or fail, which means it can catapult you forward in business or thrust you backwards as an entrepreneur and a leader. There are a multitude of ways to communicate such as verbal and non-verbal, the type of clothing used to express self, the behavior in which one acts and much more. To move past a business-owner mentality into an entrepreneurial state-of-mind, you must learn to transform your environment by being transformational in your actions, words, and behaviors and through your relationships, culture, and environments. The ultimate keys to success are simple; understand the process and learning the process; the PROCESS OF SELF! You hold the key to transforming events, situations, failures, and successes of life.

A business owner is frequently short on time and does not have enough hours in a day to deal with everything needed to successfully operate a business, however, an entrepreneur finds a way to balance home, work, schools, family, relationships, along with personal and professional success.

"In America, the problems of poverty and low income, particularly for minorities, are disproportionately focused on the inner cities. Shining a spotlight on the businesses growing in these communities is proof that any community has the potential for entrepreneurship."

-Michael Porter

DR. TEKEMIA DORSEY'S SPORTS ACADEMY 4 URBAN YOUTH

Dr. Tekemia Dorsey's Sports Academy 4 Youth is an executive leadership program for athletic and non-athletic students ages 10-16 years old. Students learn to lead through behavior, advocacy, leadership, and civic engagement.

During the covid19 pandemic, Dorsey launched a Summer Hybrid Program that rolled over into a Fall program. Topics selected for the Summer Hybrid Program and Student-Athlete Leadership Programs were instrumental in assisting the youth with a 360-degree transformation of change through behavior. These learning variables remain vital to success, especially for underserved and underrepresented youth.

Why are these components important?

Leadership Training & Development, Workforce Development Education & Certification, Career and College Readiness, and Health and Wellness and the newly added component are essential because much is unveiled for success when a dive deep into each is explored. Students do not learn these variables in a program at once. Suppose they become familiar with these topics later in life, such as 11th, 12th, or collegiate years. The latter years are too late to plant seeds and watch them blossom in youth. For youth in urban communities, the later years are too late to learn, explore, and capitalize on these variables for success in life.

Youth respond best through structure, time management, organization, and buy-in. Buy-in means having viable input where their voices are not just heard but become part of the process. Adults do so as well, but when youth can see the value of their experience and how it connects to the real world, they tend to take a greater interest in their personal and professional growth and development. Instead of youth sitting in the passenger or back seat of the process, they have the aptitude to become the driver of change if they can lead more. Youth who took part and community leaders and partners experienced the same metamorphosis experiences through the Summer/Fall programs.

Employable Skills vs. Degrees During a Pandemic

Project IABT's Summer Hybrid Program was underway. The focus of the summer experience was breaking the cycle of poverty in urban communities through the triathlon sport. What was learned from the Covid19 Pandemic was that having a degree was not sufficient. An unconventional approach was necessary to ensure urban youth did not fall beneath the poverty level, be impacted by youth unemployment by age 16, and acquire employable skills in life.

Summer Hybrid Program Expectations

1. Each program participant enrolled in a course in IABT's fundamentals workforce development academy to enhance their skill set in an area of interest to them.

2. Each program participant became a part of the subgroup entitled "Immobilizing the Troops." The Immobilizing the Troops was a youth-centered cohort subgroup that focused on leadership, accountability, and goal-oriented success within the summer and fall programs.

3. The Cohort met daily Monday – Friday, 7:30 – 10:00 am before the start of the summer hybrid program and one hour before the start of their program over the program's execution. Once the summer hybrid program launched, they met from 7:30 – 8:30 am, Monday – Friday.

4. Fundamental Course Selections for students can be viewed at https://www.ed2go.com/theiabt

5. Dr. Dorsey spoke with each program participant to identify interests and appropriate course selection on or before June 22, 2020.

These were just some of the expectations presented to the youth, and they helped tremendously guide and facilitate programming throughout the youth summer experience.

Youth engaged in a Pre-Week Orientation, and parents also went through a Parent, Youth, & Staff Kick-Off Meeting. The Pre-Week Orientation was designed to get youth acclimated to the schedule, assess their interests, discuss the program's parameters, glean their insights, etc. The Kickoff Meeting was an opportunity for youth, parents, and staff to finally meet one another and discuss upcoming experiences, expectations, questions, and answers.

The initial program was designed to focus on activities to keep the youth engaged and not bored, activities that would pique their interests and keep them on their toes. Due to a hybrid modality, there was a strong need to ensure that the youth perspective was not overwhelming and keep the youth in front of the computers for long periods, even with activities. The program schedule integrated appropriate breaks filled with various activities and engaging content. The program objectives were achieved, but adaptation was needed when the program moved from theory to practical application.

With the input of youth participants, the initial program design was adapted.

Initial Program Overview

Our summer hybrid program's focus was 50 students (middle and high) between the ages of 12 and 16 residing in under-served and under-represented communities in Baltimore County, Maryland.

Adapted Version - Program Focus

Due to its hybrid focus, the program was expanded to cover Maryland, not just Baltimore County. Students enrolled included Baltimore County, Baltimore City, and Prince Georges County, Maryland. The program included youth ages 9 - 15 years old.

Initial Program Dates

The dates of the program are June 29 – August 7, 2020. The program employed certified instructors where youth were to enhance their innate skills set, acknowledge new knowledge and certifications that would prepare them one step closer to becoming employable, and break the cycle of poverty during their summer experience.

Adapted Program Dates

The program dates spanned from June 15 - October 11, 2020 (Summer and Fall Programs).

Initial Program Design

The design included four (4) components: Leadership Training & Development Through STEM, Workforce Development Education & Certification, Career and College Readiness, and Health and Wellness.

Program Design

• Leadership Training and Development Through STEM (Hybrid)

Team Building Exercises
Communication
Portfolio Development
Cultural Diversity
Science, Technology, Engineering, and Math
Construct geodesic dome;
Construct robotic hand;
Design and test bridges;
Design and build building structures and tunnels;
Construct geodesic domes;
Construct tall towers;
Make and evaluate what makes good building material

• Career and College Readiness Exploration (Hybrid)

Exploring Job Fields
Portfolio Development
Professional Student Headshot (Youth Entrepreneur)
Resume Development
Internship Exploration
Financial Literacy

• Workforce Development Education & Certification (For those its deemed appropriate for)

Fundamental Courses (Online)
6 weeks – 24 hours of Classroom Time
Certified Instructors
Online Format
Support from Mentors from Program
Received New Skillset and Certification of Completion
Certification (Hybrid)
CPR/AED Adult/Infant Certification (all participants – virtual)
Swim Certification (Those Interested)
Track & Field Certification (Those Interested), etc

• Health & Wellness (Reducing Health Disparities Through Recreational Activity)

Learn to Swim Program (if facility opens)
Run Training (In person)
Mini Swim Clinic (if facility opens)
Mini Run Clinic (In person)
Cycle Training, plus (Hybrid)
Yoga
Strength & Conditioning
Nutrition Education

Foundational Principles

From the initial program designed viewed above, foundational principles immediately were introduced for a successful foundation to complete this comprehensive, aggressive program experience.

- Time Management & Organization
- Communication
- S.M.A.R.T. Goals
- Cohort Culture

These themes were important foundation principles to guide a positive program experience and it worked. During the Pre-Orientation Week, youth participants begin to dive into time management and organization, communication, the cohort culture, and SMART Goals. It was clear that while most youth participants were familiar with at least three of the four themes, the inconsistency was the consistency in using the concepts for success.

The culture of a cohort was new to most, but they quickly adapted to the idea and success of the program. What was important with this foundational principle was that everyone entered this program on an even platform regardless of academics, socioeconomics, physically challenged level, geographic location, age, etc. It was also a quick learning curve because understand no one was better or significant than another.

Youth participants were not only learning the foundational principles, but they were applying them in real application as each day passed by. Not all youth brought into each concept right away however by the end of Week 1 (which included the Pre-Orientation Week), it became obvious the importance each one would play for a successful program experience.

Dr. Dorsey met with each youth participant individually to explore their choice for the selection of their college course. The goal of the course selection should be a course from which the youth could envision himself or herself in, in the near future. This discussion took some exploration and deep dive on the part of the youth and Dr. Dorsey. The youth participants were now being forced to think (using analytical, logical and critical thinking infused with their current academic interests). It allowed the youth participants to also look beyond their current grade level and age to the possibilities of life.

Each of the youth participants were able to make a choice that aligned with their future goals. There were youth that changed their minds mid-program and changed into a new course. When this happened, real world application was applied to the discussion. High School youth enter college with a goal in mind and that remains graduation. Often than not, youth do not take the time to fully explore their majors before selecting and when that happens, people graduate from college unable to work in the field from which their degree is awarded. They ae also in debt and jobless.

As each youth participant engaged in their college courses, and other concepts of their program experience, their thinking, actions, and views begin to shift. They begin to BELIEVE in what seemed to be the impossible. The begin to not just hold self and other cohort accountable for their actions. The accountabilities were simple which included but were not limited to, (1) showing up on time (2) not being late from break (3) cameras on and (4) everyone being active during the session. The further in the program weeks continued the less distractions there were.

Adapted Program Design

As we approached vital aspects of the program that fell under Workforce Development and Career & College Readiness, working with the students, Dorsey became stuck in their efforts. Dorsey encounter roadblocks with programming because the student participants lacked the necessary tools for success. The lack of essential tools was a concern for at least 85% of the participants and a massive problem for moving to the next program objective. The geographic location of the students was an irrelevant factor. It was a cultural infringement that needed addressing. Despite having participants from three of the state's largest cities, the majority's underlying concern was the same.

Given the roadblock provided during one of the main program objectives, a program component was added. The new feature was called the Student-Athlete Leadership Program. This new feature falls within Dr. Tekemia Dorsey's Sports Academy 4 Urban Youth. With the new feature and its purpose, the summer hybrid program now rolled over into the Fall.

Fall Program Experience

Adapted Program Design

The program designed included a fifth component to the Summer Hybrid Program experience and the Fall Program was launched. The fifth component focused on Community Service, Service Learning, and Civic Engagement. Student participants were learning through knowledge and experience the importance of advocacy, networking, marketing, leadership, program design, program implementation, personal growth, and development.

The Student-Athlete Leadership Program was charged with advocating, leading, and giving back to their communities. Together the Student-Athlete Leadership Program cohort brainstormed, planned, and implemented TRIAD Program Initiatives for underserved and underrepresented youth and communities.

Our Student-Athlete Leaders completed an 8-week comprehensive Leadership Training and Development through STEM, Career and College Readiness, Workforce Development, Education and Certification, and Health and Wellness Program. In turn, they designed and executed triad initiatives of giving back.

The International Association of Black Triathletes (IABT) - Student-Athlete Leadership Hybrid Program participants hosted three initiatives for youth and families from underserved and underrepresented communities. The triad initiatives were:

1. Holiday Drive
2. 5K Run/Walk Virtual Fundraiser
3. Health & Wellness Community Giveback Event

The Holiday Drive was designed to collect coats, hats, gloves, scarfs, and socks for underserved and underrepresented youth and families.

The 5K Run/Walk - Virtual Edition was a fundraising initiative for the Health and Wellness Community Giveback Event. Raise funds while fighting the health disparities commonly known in urban communities (childhood and adult obesity and cancer). The goal was to get youth and adults from deprived communities (all cities) moving and engaging.

They desired to share and to pass on blessings bestowed to them. Their Health & Wellness Community Giveback Event occurred on Saturday, September 26, 2020, from 10 am - 12:30 pm, in partnership with D4G Creative Arts Center. IABT's Student-Athlete Leaders adopted Destined 4 Greatness Learning Center students and other youth for this event.

With these TRIAD Program Initiatives, they focused on unborn youth to seniors within a 7-week time spanned. While successfully completely the TRIAD Program Initiatives, they were building their resume, portfolios, scholarship opportunities, and received a HUGE set of acknowledgments in the end.

Summation

In urban communities, there are many barriers urban youth and families face that continue to impede quality and longevity in life. In metropolitan cities, issues such as poverty, education, college and career readiness, workforce development readiness, lack of being employable and marketable, health and wellness, intervention and postvention versus prevention are adversities faced, along with transportation, institutional racism, gender bias, lack of opportunities, lack of privilege, lack of resources, lack of finances, and the list continues.

Although these barriers, obstacles, and adversities will continue to exist, there are solutions to address these concerns and close the gaps. The multisport industry is a unique, powerful, and diverse one as it universal to all. Urban youth need an outlet that allows them to be them unapologetically. Dorsey's Transformational Leadership Model utilizing multisport industry as part of the foundation under The International Association of Triathletes (IABT)'s umbrella, where all children can grow in self as needed, providing tools necessary and required as prevention to success provides change needed for urban youth, urban communities, and their urban futures.

Organizational Impact

We set out to achieve the following during our Covid19 Hybrid Program:

• At least 80% of participants will increase their employability skills.

• At least 50% of participants will possess tools for success in college and career exploration.

- At least 75% of participants will exit with certifications in areas that will enhance their skill sets and marketability.

- Participants will learn how to decrease the health disparity levels within their households.

- Participants will develop strategies to reduce and to manage stress.

- Participants will learn to become leaders in life, workplace settings, and their communities.

We achieved the following:

- 100% of participants learned how to decrease the health disparity levels within their households.

- 100% of participants developed strategies to reduce and to manage stress.

- 100% of participants learned to become leaders in life, workplace settings, and their communities.95% of participants will increase their employability skills.

- 95% of participants will possess tools for success in college and career exploration.

- 95% of participants exited with certifications in areas that will enhance their skill sets and marketability

- 90% of participants brainstormed, executed, and successfully implemented TRIAD Initiative Programs for underserved and underrepresented communities and received recognition from Baltimore City Mayor Young, Baltimore County Executive John Olszewski, Jr. and state of Maryland, Governor Hogan.

- 90% of participants became CPR/AED Adult, Child and Infant Certified.

- 90% of participants created resumes and developed portfolios.

- 90% of participants successfully completed college-level courses.

- 90% of participants successfully took part in financial literacy.

- 90% of participants sat for Professional Headshots.

- 90% of participants learned advocacy, increased their leadership and personal growth and development.

- 90% of participants earned at least 50 hours of service-learning hours that go towards graduation requirements.

- 90% of participants acquired letters of recommendation for their portfolio and scholarship applications.

- 90% of participants begin college and career readiness, internships, job exploration, college majors, etc.

- 90% of participants begin college and career readiness, internships, job exploration, college majors, etc.

- 90% of participants graduated from our DTD's Sports Academy 4 Urban Youth.

URBAN YOUTH PERSPECTIVE

1. Who Am I? - At the beginning of the program, of those enrolled, only a handful of youth were comfortable in sharing who they were. As you can imagine, from a youth perspective, most had not considered who they were. They were clear (most anyway) in their likes and dislikes, and some were quite uncertain. The significant part of exploring this topic during the program experience is that the youth participants remained open and optimistic to understand what they had yet to learn.

2. Critical Thinking – during the program experiences, youth participants were required to think and act through the process, individually and collectively. Youth participants were introduced to concepts, content, theories, and subjects they were and were not familiar with. Although variables were familiar to them, the curriculum allowed them to see the concepts individually and as part of a process. Youth participants were able to create a blueprint that will assist them in any stage of life, regardless of industry or interests.

3. Team Building – during the program experiences, youth participants participated in team-building activities from the start to the end. From their summer program experience through the fall program experience. It was amazing to see them bond on various levels despite the culturally diverse barriers that presented themselves. Youth from across the state of Maryland from a dichotomy of backgrounds and influences had come together like a cohesive unit by the end. They were family. They were leaders in their community that achieved during a pandemic that most had not achieved in normal circumstances. Youth participants worked on several projects over the summer and fall program experiences that included brainstorming, developing, and implementing webinar presentations and ongoing in-person projects for the community.

4. Cultural Diversity – during the program experiences, youth participants overcame internal and external aspects of cultural diversity. Youth participants' ages ranged from 9 – 15 years old. Youth participants included mainstreamed youth as well as those with disabilities. Those that were SPEC Needs fell in the categories of Asperger's, ADD/ADHD, and a Neurological Tick Disorder. Youth participants evolved from different socioeconomic backgrounds, including Baltimore County, Baltimore City, and Prince Georges County, MD. Youth participants' grade levels included elementary, middle, and high school. Youth participants were from private and public-school settings and magnet school programs. Youth participants were introduced to various topics from various instructors in various

modalities of delivery.

5. Real World Events – during the program experiences, youth participants were introduced to real-world events. Youth participants took part in certifications such as CPR/AED and Adult, Infant, and Children training. They all became certified.

a. Youth participants all took part in sitting for Professional Headshots to develop the portfolios. Youth participants took part in financial literacy workshop with PNC Bank.

b. Youth participants took part in resume writing. Youth participants took part in writing the request Letters of Recommendations.

c. Youth participants took part in Collegiate Level courses, and some sat for their exams at the end. Youth participants selected collegiate courses, and some realized the course was too hard. Unlike the real-world scenarios and real-world scenarios, youth participants were able to drop that course and enroll in another collegiate course.

d. Youth participants were able to network with industry leaders, local council members, etc. Youth participants learned that every person, regardless of race, goes through things in life, and where they end is not what they may have considered as options.

e. Youth participants learned from guest speakers that they did not necessarily come from money; they were not perfect youth and had gone through troubled times and unconventional pathways, but they continued to PUSH despite their upbringing FORWARD to improve their lives.

f. Youth participants also learned that many commonalities of the guest speakers were that they came into their career pathways later in life through various ways but most importantly, not allowing their circumstances as youth be the determining factor of what their futures could or can be.

g. Youth participants engaged in the brainstorming, development, and execution of several presentations for the general public, including parents, families, and friends of their newly acquired skillsets and community service TRIAD initiatives.

6. Leadership Attributes – during the program experiences, each youth participant arrived at the table with innate leadership abilities and attributes; however, they could not identify their leadership traits. At this stage in their

lives, it is widespread for youth to be unable to identify what leadership is and what leadership traits they possess. This is also a HUGE disparity that needs to be changed immediately.

a. Youth participants soon begin to understand the answer to Who Am I? The answers to these questions begin to unveil their innate leadership skills, traits, and abilities. Youth participants begin to embrace the idea and the truth that they are remarkable human beings with untapped potential and talent awaiting the unveiling within their lives.

b. Youth participants infused with real-world scenarios during the program experiences such as the death of George Floyd, John Lewis, and the Black Lives Matter moments learned a lot about the world's past, present, and future. History repeats itself, and minorities are based on race, gender, creed, religion, socioeconomic status, geographic location, and even disability.

c. Youth participants unveiled and acquired new leadership traits, skill sets, and abilities. Examples of leadership traits developed and mastered throughout program experiences include public speaking, creating and executing presentations and technology, networking, program creation, program execution, teamwork, the list continues, etc. Through a change in behavior, mindset, and outlook on life, youth participants completed leadership training and applied those same leadership skills in the community.

7. Communication – during the program experiences, communication was a skill that youth participants learned to grow into, develop more, and learned to master for success at that stage in their lives.

A. Youth participants are not as vocal in expression as the world would like during the age range of 9-15; however, their communications skills changed dramatically during their training.

b. Youth participants could not communicate with non-verbal gestures as they are often used to doing. Youth participants could no longer use "I don't know" or "No" to answer an inquiry or communicate with others.

c. Youth participants learned to use their voice for more than what they were familiar with, and what they understood, in the end, was that advocacy is the best approach to life. Advocacy is a form of communication that change the trajectory of their lives and the lives of others.

d. Youth participants embraced advocacy to its fullest extent by the end of their program experiences. Their end of the program's success reinforces such outcomes.

8. Be Transformational – during the program experiences, youth participants were unaware of the transformation and manifestation within self that was to take place. With any program youth participants participate in, they should exit a different person. Youth participants went through a metamorphosis by the end of the program experiences. Metamorphosis is a change of the form or nature of a thing or person into a completely different one by natural or supernatural means.

9. 360 Degree Transformation – The 360-degree transformation occurs when the participant demonstrates a change in mental, physical, intellect, and behavior.

Special Needs Population

Youth who fall within the special needs population is no different in training and preparation requirements from students who reside in mainstream classrooms or even access to sports, including those who participate in the multisport industry.

Youth, in general, are born with genetic markers passed down to them from their parents, their parents – parents and even some that skip a generation or two or three, etc. Some youth experience acknowledgment of their disability earlier in life and others later in life. No one truly knows when a disability decides to rear its ugly head for diagnosis or due to mild to severe symptoms. There are many such disabilities that it is difficult to concretely identify patterns, signs, etc., for every diagnosis at a certain point in life.

Despite the disability a youth is born with, or that develops over one lifespan, opportunities in life are still required for positive growth and development. The opportunities such as education, sports, training, preparation, etc., remain required but may have to be modified or adapted. What does not have to be modified or adapted in life is advocacy and leadership to improve ones' circumstances and overall contributions to self and *be* an asset to society. Training and preparation through programs and services should be introduced as soon as a youth is able. When training and preparation through programs and services are not introduced earlier on in life, a lack of success and progression is expected.

Key transition skills

It can be argued that students who do not have or manage to develop the critical transition skills are less likely to transition into, thrive, and transition with qualifications out of higher education. Thus, poor transition leads to non-continuation and non-completion of degrees. Yorke and Longden found that 'the major influences on non-continuation continued to be a poor choice of the program; lack of personal commitment to study; teaching quality; lack of contact with academic staff; inadequate academic progress; and finance' (Yorke, 2008, p.2).

Jones (2008) listed some overlapping factors as contributing to early withdrawal:

- preparation for higher education
- institutional and course match
- academic experience
- social integration
- financial issues
- personal circumstances.

Although many of the influences and factors identified in the literature are the responsibility of the student and their ability to manage their transition, Tinto recognized that institutions also had to accept some responsibility. He proposed that there should be a reflection on the design of the 'educational conditions in which we place students' (Tinto, 2009, p. 2). He concluded that five educational conditions that institutions could design into the student experience stood out: commitment, expectations, support, feedback, and involvement.

One study proposed that student engagement was a critical factor in successful transition and that this lies on a continuum from disengaged to engaged. This research also revealed shared responsibility between the student and the institution. It concluded that 'students are more likely to engage if they, in turn, are supported by teaching staff who engage with students, with the subject, and with the teaching process (Bryson & Hand, 2007, p. 349).

Gale found that a significant amount of early transition support promoted the idea of students adapting to fit into higher education. He observed that central support in higher education existed not primarily to develop the learner's skills but to help students adapt to the institution (Gale, 2009). This model is insufficient where the principle is about engaging with difference. When considering different transition models, Gale suggests considering 'the creation of space in higher education not just for new kinds of student bodies but also for their embodied pieces of knowledge and ways of knowing' (Gale 2009, p. 14).

With an opportunity to be part of the process, i.e., planning, brainstorming, training, and leading the charge, youth within the special needs' population will be able to advocate for themselves, avoid the poverty pitfalls of life and have a greater chance at being productive members of society. The problem is that not enough youth with disabilities are provided an opportunity of inclusion for advancement where they are treated as equals in the process as opposed to being told what to do. There lies a massive disparity in ownership, accountability, understanding, and execution from one youth perspective.

Dr. Tekemia's Dorsey's (DTD) Sports Academy 4 Urban Youth

As a part of the Dr. Tekemia Dorsey's (DTD) Sports Academy 4 Urban Youth (Class of 2020), youth from all urban walks were welcomed. During the Case Study presented, two participants were youth who fell within the special **needs'** population. Despite their limitations in some ways, they were able to complete the program and curriculum without any adaptations, just as the mainstream youth did. During both the Fall and the Spring programs, these youth were successful from beginning to end and contributed significantly.

One youth, age 12, was a male with a neurological tick disorder. According to CDC.gov, Neurological "Tics are sudden twitches, movements, or sounds that people repeatedly do. People who have tics cannot stop their bodies from doing these things. For example, a person with a motor tic might keep blinking repeatedly, or a person with a vocal tic might make a grunting sound unwillingly" (https://www.cdc.gov). The 12-year-old had just completed sixth grade and had competed in triathlons for the last six years.

The other youth at the time, age 14 and a male, had Asperger's, Autism, and Adhd. According to the Autism website, "Asperger syndrome generally involves Difficulty with social interactions; Restricted interests; Desire for sameness; Distinctive strengths" (www.autismspeaks.org). Autism is "a developmental disorder of variable severity characterized by difficulty in social interaction and communication and by restricted or repetitive patterns of thought and behavior" (Dictionary.com).

ADHD is defined as "ADHD is one of the most common neurodevelopmental disorders of childhood. It is usually first diagnosed in childhood and often lasts into adulthood. Children with ADHD may have trouble paying attention, controlling impulsive behaviors (may act without thinking about what the result will be), or be overly active" (www.cdc.gov).

A chronic condition includes attention difficulty, hyperactivity, and impulsiveness. ADHD often begins in childhood and can persist into adulthood. It may contribute to low self-esteem, troubled relationships, and difficulty at school or work. Symptoms include limited attention and hyperactivity. Treatments include medication and talk therapy (www.cdc.gov). This 14-year-old had just completed 8th grade. He is also a fraternal twin. He is not a triathlete but has just begun training to become a triathlete with the IABT Junior Multisport Club.

Advocacy, Leadership, and Breaking The Cycle of Poverty Through The Triathlon Sport

Youth who participated in the summer and fall programs through the Dr. Tekemia Dorsey's Sports Academy 4 Urban Youth experienced a unique, comprehensive, and unique program. The critical factors of the program were buy-in, such as student involvement, student accountability, student feedback, student program design, and the list continue. While the program was created around the student, once the program started with their feedback, tweaks were able to ensure maximum productivity and quality outcomes (See Case Study summary). There are tools to assist with success during and after high school for youth who fall within the special **needs'** population across the United States who may or may not be engaged in programs such as Dr. Tekemia Dorsey's Sports Academy 4 Urban Youth.

Parents are often uncertain what their options are when their youth grades begin to decline, an increase of assignments is missing, and when students' behavior begins to change, shift, or become irregular. It's difficult for warning signs to be different from usual teenage stuff, but it is pretty different. As a matter of reference, when a youth begins to change or shift in or towards school, that is a clear sign that something is going on. Often, it is not caught early enough until the youth behavior evolves into a disciplinary concern.

A change in a youth's behavior is not the only indicator of youth struggling academically. Other signs are dwindling grades, missing assignments, and even low grades on assignments. Youth do not want to be viewed as dumb, unique, or want help right away. Most of the time, they want to at least try it on their own.

In the multisport industry, youth with and without a disability can glean confidence, self-esteem, and certainty of self as they train and compete. Junior Triathlete, BJ Simons, who lives daily with a neurological tick disorder, says, "Triathlons is his Superpower and helps him feel normal" (Simons & Simons, 2020). Junior Triathlon, Halz Simons, who has a 504 Plan for accommodations due to vision concerns in education, has benefited from the triathlon sport to become the First African American Youth Triathlete turned Business Owner in the country (Simons & Simons, 2020).

There are options for parents and youth with disabilities to assist in their educational endeavors. Options include a 504 plan, an Individual Education Plan, and an Individual Transition Plan. These options provide accommodations for youth with disabilities in the classroom and can be a source of awareness for youth in all areas of life.

Junior Triathlete Halz S. 504 plan provides accommodations for vision concerns that address concerns educationally. External from the 504 plan educationally, the vision concerns experienced during training and competing have been addressed through prescription swim goggles, prescription glasses, and prescription sports glasses. As a result of the medical condition with her vision, Halz S.'s training, competition, and educational disparities have been accommodated for continued success.

There is a direct correlation and impact of concerns on and off the field with urban youth in the triathlon sport. There is a direct correlation and impact with solutions on and off the field with urban youth in the triathlon sport.

Education & Post-Secondary Plan Options

These education and post-secondary plan options are not presented in any particular order.

504 Plan

Section 504 defines an "individual with a disability" broadly as "Any person who (1) has a physical or mental impairment which substantially limits one or more of such person's major life activities; (2) has a record of such an impairment; or (3) is regarded as having such an impairment." What does this mean?

Your child must have a legal disability to get a 504 plan. (Kids who learn or think differently generally do.) Start by gathering any documents about your child's needs, like any records of a medical diagnosis. Other things to gather are schoolwork, report cards, and private evaluations.

A student must have a specific medical diagnosis to be considered for Section §504. There is no legal basis under 504 to require a medical diagnosis. However, evaluation processes would typically need to be more thorough and involved if this information does not exist.

For a child who is having trouble in school, a 504 plan can offer a lot of support. The plan can put in place changes to how your child is taught, like frequent breaks or audiobooks. 504 plans are great for kids who do not need but who do need support to learn.

How do you get your child a 504 plan?

Many kids get a 504 plan after they are found not eligible for an IEP. When this happens, the school usually proposes the plan. Other times, though, families ask the school for a 504 plan. If that is you, here are seven steps to get your child a 504 plan.

1. Document your child's needs.

Your child must have a legal to get a 504 plan. (Kids who learn or think differently generally do.) Start by gathering any documents about your child's needs, like any records of a medical diagnosis. Other things to gather are schoolwork, report cards, and private evaluations. It can be helpful to organize these papers in a binder.

2. Find out who the school's 504 coordinator is.

Every public school district must have a staff member who coordinates 504 plans. This person may also be the IEP coordinator. Check the school website for the coordinator's name and contact information. If you can't find it, ask the principal.

3. Write a formal request for a 504 plan.

You will need to make a formal written request for a 504 plan. Use this sample letter as a model. In your request, be specific about why you're asking for the plan. For example, you might say: "I would like a 504 plan for my child who, due to, needs frequent breaks throughout the day to be able to learn like his peers."

4. Follow up on your request.

The 504 coordinators should respond right away. However, you can keep things on track by following up by email or phone after a few days.

5. Go through the 504-plan evaluation process.

An evaluation for a 504 plan is not always as comprehensive as one for an IEP. But the school will still want to review your child's schoolwork, medical records, and other documents. The school will also want to talk with and observe your child, as well as interview you, your child's teacher, and other school staff.

6. Meet with the school to see if your child qualifies.

After the evaluation, the school will most likely meet with you to decide if your child qualifies. You can also ask for this meeting if the school doesn't schedule it. If your child qualifies, you will move to the next step. If not, it may be time to look at your options for 504 plan dispute resolution.

7. Work together to create the 504 Plan.

Once your child qualifies for a 504 plan, the school will work with you to create the plan. A written 504 plan is not required. But most schools will create one. Download a sample 504 plan to see what it might look like. And get tips for developing a good 504 plan.

Keep in mind that another way to get a 504 plan is through the standard IEP process. That is why if you are not sure whether your child needs an IEP or a 504 plan, it may be best to request an evaluation for an IEP.

Individual Education Plan (IEP)

An Individualized Education Plan (or Program) is also known as an IEP. This is a plan or program developed to ensure that a child with an identified disability who is attending an elementary or secondary educational institution receives specialized instruction and related services.

All students need guidance in order to make the leap from high school to the next step. Students with learning disabilities, however, need even more help because their leap is that much greater. The IEP transition plan ensures not only that these children will be able to function as adults in the real world but to also increase the likelihood they will pursue post-secondary education. As it stands now, those rates are dismal: only 13 percent of students with learning disabilities make it to post-secondary education, as compared to 53 percent of the general population.

In other words, the IEP transition plan goes beyond simply finding a place for LD students after high school. It provides a personalized course of action based on students' strengths, desires, and dreams for a fulfilling life.

Individual Transition Plan (ITP)

According to IDEA, a transition plan is required for students enrolled in special education who have an Individualized Education Program (IEP). This individual transition plan is known as an ITP. The ITP is a section of the IEP that outlines transition goals and services for the student with disability. The IDEA requires that all students must have an ITP by the age of 14 but no later than age 16. Unfortunately, Heaven is almost 17 and her ITP still needs to be completed, especially with APPLA part of her permanency plan under DSS. According to DSS plan of action, independent living (APPLA) can begin for Heaven once she turns 17 in October, however being a teen with an IEP and mental health diagnosis, an ITP must be in place and activated.

Individualized Transition Plan, or ITP, is a plan based on informal and formal assessments that is used to identify the desired and expected outcomes by students and their families once they leave school as well as the supports needed to achieve these outcomes.

What types of assessments are used to develop the transition plan?

Types of transition assessments include:

1. behavioral assessment information,

2. aptitude tests, interest, and work values inventories,
3. intelligence tests and achievement tests,
4. personality or preference tests,
5. career maturity or readiness tests,
6. self-determination assessments,
7. work-related temperament scales, and
8. transition ... (including APPLA through DSS).

The IDEA recognizes the importance of preparing youth for success after high school and states that transition planning for students who receive special education services and have an Individualized Education Program (IEP) must begin by age 14.

The four principal components of a Transition Planning Project Plan are:

1) Task Identification and Schedule Development,
2) Transition Committee Deployment and Support,
3) Occupancy and Activation Planning; and
4) Move Planning.

Key Elements to the Transition Planning and the IEP

- Age-Appropriate Transition Assessment (AATA)
- Student Vision.
- Post-Secondary Goals.
- Course of study.
- Transition services.
- Agencies and providers.
- Annual goals.

What is secondary transition and why is it important for students with disabilities?

Students with learning disabilities, however, need even more help because their leap is that much greater. The IEP transition plan ensures not only that these children will be able to function as adults in the real world but to also increase the likelihood they will pursue post-secondary education.

Why Is Transition Planning Important in Special Education?

Life is never stagnant — we are all transitioning at one time or another. For the special needs child, however, "transition" has a very specific meaning. It is part of the overall Individualized Education Program, or IEP, and it defines the move from public school to adult life. The IEP transition plan, as it is called, is required by law for students with a learning disability.

What Is Transition Planning?

The law that governs the individualized transition plan is the Individuals with Disabilities Education Act (IDEA), which is in alignment with the No Child Left Behind Act. As stated in the IDEA, transition services are to be available as part of the IEP. This includes assessments of the child by a team, resulting in goal setting in the following areas:

- Training.
- Education.
- Employment.
- Independent living skills if necessary.

Schools must offer transition services leading to fulfillment of these goals, which must be set by the time the child reaches age 16. That means transition planning really starts before the child turns 16. In some states, the IEP transition plan is required by an even earlier age. Texas, for example, requires a transition plan by the age of 14.

The needs of the student, the relevant goals, and the plan of action for his or her school to fulfill those goals must all be documented and kept on file at the school. Schools must report to parents on the progress of the student towards meeting those transition goals.

Why is Transition Planning Important?

It is not enough to simply be aware that teenagers need guidance to transition successfully from high school to the next phase of young adulthood; concrete action steps must be taken to guide and prepare teens for college and/or a career, and for independent living. Without this guidance, students with learning disabilities often fail or flounder in high school and beyond. Consider these sobering statistics:

- Over 30% of children with learning disabilities drop out of high school. (Source: 28th Annual Report to Congress on the Implementation of the Individuals with Disabilities Education Act, 2006)

- Only 13% of students with learning disabilities (compared to 53% of students in the general population) have attended a 4-year post-secondary school program within two years of leaving high school. (Source: National Longitudinal Transition Study, 1994)

What are specific transition services examples?

WHAT ARE TRANSITION SERVICES? school to post-school activities, including postsecondary education; vocational education; integrated employment (including supported employment); continuing and adult education; adult services; independent living; or community participation.

What are transition skills?

The main transition skills identified were self-efficacy (re-named as 'self-belief' following feedback from student focus groups); critical self-reflection; independent learning; self-management of expectations; social skills; dealing with stress; critical thinking; academic; and information literacy.

What are the most important factors in determining the success of an individualized transition plan?

The most successful transition plans have all the critical elements, including education goals, independent living goals, and a coordinated effort to achieve these goals. Successful transition plans include a student's preferences, interests, and personal needs.

What is the difference between a postsecondary and an annual transition goal?

Postsecondary goals capture students' visions of adult life, whereas annual goals address the means by which students access the secondary school coursework and other educational experiences that will enable them to successfully pursue their postsecondary goals.

What types of organizations must be included in the transition plan to support the student's goals?

This would include representatives from school-to-work transition programs, local social service agencies, counseling programs, medical care providers, and advocates. Parents are key players in the transition planning process.

What IDEA says about transition planning?

The IDEA recognizes the importance of preparing youth for success after high school and states that transition planning for students who receive special education services and have an Individualized Education Program (IEP) must begin by age 16 (some states require that the process starts earlier). A transition plan is required for students enrolled in special education who have an Individualized Education Program (IEP).

"*Federal law for special education requires that high schools help students and families develop transition plan*," Shattuck adds. But that does not always happen. *Only 58 percent of high school students with autism had a transition plan by age 14, as required by federal law.* "That's a big accountability problem," Shattuck says.

A transition plan is the section of the Individualized Education Program (IEP) that outlines transition goals and services for the student. ... Transition planning is used to identify and develop goals which need to be accomplished during the current school year to assist the student in meeting his post-high school goals.

What is transition planning in school?

Transition planning is a coordinated set. of activities which promote a student's movement from high school to postsecondary education or employment and independent living. Transition planning is based on the individual student's interests, strengths, and needs.

What is transition planning and why is it important?

Transition planning is the key to making school relevant to your child's future life as an adult. Together, the IEP team and your child will set postsecondary goals, choose activities, and connect with the necessary resources and services.

What is the purpose of the individual transition plan?

Individualized Transition Plan, or ITP, is a plan based on informal and formal assessments that is used to identify the desired and expected outcomes by students and their families once they leave school as well as the supports needed to achieve these outcomes.

Working with urban youth, urban families, and urban communities, it is vital to understand not just the barriers that impeded success, along with the solutions to address them but to simply acknowledge, circumstances are quite different than the normal. When a holistic approach is utilized, success is imminent for all, especially the youth. The triathlon sport provides a strong foundation for urban youth but other barriers with this targeted population need addressing that goes far beyond a sport.

The special needs population can appear as a barrier to work with however this population are blessings in disguise and teach leaders and other participants how to truly see life as it is. Understanding how to navigate barriers with persons, especially urban youth that are different increases the society's chances of a better future.

SPECIAL ED TRANSITION PLANNING: FIVE KEYS TO SUCCESS

Best Practices to Guarantee Student Success and Federal Requirement Compliance

The federal government has handed down an ultimatum: meet required performance indicators and graduation rates for special education students or face the consequences.

It's a pain school district administrator are very familiar with — they feel it every day. When districts are not in compliance, it is top level administrators who are ultimately held accountable.

How can district administrators ensure best practices are being implemented at the school level? How can they guarantee student performance improvement and alignment with compliance regulations?

The challenge is meeting the needs at the federal, state, district, school, classroom, and student level — but simply meeting compliance requirements isn't enough. Teachers can do everything required to be compliant and still not improve graduation rates or post-secondary outcomes for special education students. Compliance is the first step, but it does not guarantee success.

Transition planning is more than a name for the age-old challenge of helping special education students plan for life after K-12. Today, it is a federal requirement with performance metrics that elevate the issue from a special education challenge to one that schools, districts and states are now evaluated on and accountable for.

Districts are charged with improving transition planning in their schools and, ultimately, improving overall student performance. But where do we start? How can districts engage teachers and deploy best practices in the classroom — all while documenting the process and remaining in compliance with federal requirements?

A New Initiative

Most administrators understand what is required for compliance, but obtaining this compliance remains a challenge.

Professional educators have seen many "initiatives" come and go. Many teachers already have an established way of creating individualized education plans for students — with differing degrees of success — and yet another requirement that must be documented and measured can be met with some resistance.

In the past, Individualized Education Plans (IEPs) and transition planning teams were two separate entities, not always working in tandem. Today, there is a new approach to the process. The most successful transition plans involve everyone in the process including IEP and transition planning teams, as well as the students themselves.

Five Keys to Successful Transition Planning

The most successful transition plans have all the critical elements, including education goals, independent living goals, and a coordinated effort to achieve these goals.

1: Student Involvement

Successful transition plans include a student's preferences, interests, and personal needs. Research shows that when students are involved in their own transition planning process, they develop a critical sense of self-awareness that helps them understand their individual needs.

Getting students involved in the process will bring forth their preferences and help them articulate what they want to achieve.

2: Self-advocacy

When students become involved in the process and develop self-awareness, they are then able to understand the different components of their individual education plans. When they start to understand these components — and can recognize their individual strengths and weaknesses — they are better positioned to self-advocate for their success.

Students who can successfully self-advocate can more effectively participate in their planning meetings, ultimately adding value to the plan itself.

Historically, many guidance counselors did not take an active role in the post-secondary goals of special education students because these students were largely contained in special education programs. Today, special education is tracked and measured, and school districts are responsible for the success of these students. The emphasis of the federal law on participation and progress in the general education program has raised the stakes for all involved in the education process for students with disabilities.

Students must stand up for themselves and advocate for their own futures. They must approach their guidance counselors and say, "I am going to college, and I need your help to get me there!"

3: Goal Setting

Goal setting is what a student lends to the process for educational and employment goals and is critical to his overall success.

Often, professionals set all of the goals and impose them on students without involving the student or asking for input. When students are involved in the process from the beginning and able to articulate what they want to accomplish, they are more likely to stay committed to obtaining their goals.

4: Self-monitoring

When students set their own goals and are in charge of monitoring their progress, they become accountable.

For example, say a student sets the goal of becoming a teacher. His/her transition plan maps out what is needed in order to accomplish this goal, including earning a four-year degree.

In order to reach this goal, the student knows that it is critical to:

- Meet with the guidance counselor,
- Create a plan to graduate from high school, and
- Be accepted by a four-year college.

Transition plans provide students with a way to monitor themselves to ensure that they earn the credits they need in order to reach their individual education goals. Students who are involved in the process from the beginning are better positioned to ask for help along the way in order to achieve these goals.

5: Self-determination

All of these best practices ultimately lead to the concept of self-determination, the idea of determining what you will be, where you will go and why.

The academic world has adopted the word "self-determination" to refer to students becoming involved in their own post-secondary education and employment plans and ultimately, determining their own futures.

The compliance elements of the recent legislation suggest this — the challenge is making it happen. Ultimately, best practices — if they occur at the classroom level — will address a district's compliance requirements. The key is to document the process and keep everyone on track.

Conclusion

Remember: the five best practices for successful transition planning are:

- Student Involvement
- Self-advocacy
- Goal Setting
- Self-monitoring
- Self-determination

Student involvement is absolutely critical to success. Involve students in the process in a documented way to help them succeed, while at the same time ensuring that your district meets compliance requirements.

BECOME A CORPORATE EXECUTIVE

To become a corporate executive, it takes a skill set beyond the ordinary employee or office worker. One has to be sharp in areas of life that are not part of the normal but the exception. To become a corporate executive, you must first know what you are working with (strengths) and things you must improve upon (weaknesses). To become a corporate executive, you must be able to step outside of your comfort zone to be successful. To be a corporate executive you cannot be humble or shallow when being criticize or receiving critique from others.

To be a corporate executive there are a few do's and don't's you should consider for success:

Don't's

1. Do Not Procrastinate

    a. Top Level Executives are not procrastinators in life but are truly meticulous in what they do and how it is done.

2. Do Not Be Fearful

    a. Top Level Executives are not fearful in taking risks or beyond the status quo to go around what they want.

    b. TLE's are not fearful of the unknown but allow it to motivate and inspire them to achieve their ultimate goals.

    c. TLE's are not fearful of appearing vulnerable and not all knowing. In order to surround yourself with the best, you can not appear as the master of all things.

3. Do Not Be Full of Doubt

    a. Top Level Executives do not doubt the impact that can make when they stay in their respective lanes.

    b. Top Level Executive value themselves more than others because only they know what their strengths and areas of weaknesses are.

4. Do Not Do Tomorrow What Needs To Be Done Today

a. Top Level Executives work long hours because they cannot afford to put off today that can be done tomorrow. This requires sacrifice and dedication to the position, to the cause, to your mission.

5. Do Not Communicate Poorly

   a. Top Level Executives speak succinctly to others and their bottom-line language caters on the ROI (return on investment) syndrome. Do not poorly communicate your intentions or what you want others to know. To become a top-level executive, you must become less wordy in discussion and more focus on the bottom line.

Do's

1. Know Your Self

   a. Top Level Executives do not allow their weaknesses outshine their strengths. Achieving any goal in life or not is largely based on knowing self, knowing your strengths and areas of improvement. However, that is far from enough to get where you want to go. In knowing yourself you must know the "internal and external" and examine these two categories of life daily.

   i. Internal

      1. What is that one thing in life that brings you happiness and peace?

      2. How do you balance a Winning Schedule?

      3. At what time of the day, are you at your best?

      4. How do you balance life and work and family?

   ii. External

      1. What resources do you have in terms of people do you have to turn to for assistance?

      2. What do you do to ease stress related situations?

3. What foundational principles help to drive your motivation daily?

2. Identify Successful Characteristics of a Leader

   a. Top Level Executives align themselves with greatness by surrounding self with those that have what they desire. To be the best, you must learn from the best and those better than him/her. As a result, you are encouraged to identify leaders around you that you want to mimic.

   b. Learn to be charismatic and transformational versus transactional and authoritative. Be solution-oriented and task driven. Understand there is a solution for every problem presented.

3. Work Smart and Not Hard

To ascend to the level of top executives, you must understand the process outweighs the outcome. Learn the process of other success top executives. Learn the system and then allow the system to work for you.

There are going to be pieces of the whole sum that are attractive to you and other pieces that are not. There may be pieces of 2-3 systems discovered that are appealing…..take those pieces and create your own but….

The point remains plan your work and work your plan. Do not attempt to go this journey without being equip with tools for success.

4. Reach Across the Party Lines

To ascend to the level of top executive, you have to play with the big dogs. Meaning you are smart, wise, and good at something and while that's great, it is not good enough therefore you must surround yourself with people smarter, wiser, and better at their craft than you are.

Don't be afraid to reach out to others who you necessarily do not agree with because that will be the very person you will learn the most from.

5. Build Rapport and Strong Relations

To ascend to the level of top executive, learn how to effectively communicate and build relationships, not relationships based off of what you are going or attempt to get from it. On the contrary, a relationship that sustain the test of time and that you leave and re-enter on good terms is a relationship worth growing and keeping.

Don't allow your inadequacies such as ego, bias, prejudice, misperception, or misunderstanding keep you from blessing others and being blessed.

To be a top level executive you have to know who you are, what you want, how you are going to get it, who is going to help you get it, what will you be required to learn in the process to grow, what motivations will be present to keep you focused and determined; what skills set are needed for success, how will you communicate along the way, how do you take your POWER and use it for good and finally arrived at the final destination determined for you, TOP LEVEL EXECUTIVE.

THE BALANCING ACT FOR MOMS

Not everyone is meant to be a mom or blessed with kids. To be a mom you must be extraordinary in nature, and you must learn that as a mom, you develop a selfish character about yourself. To be a mom, you must consistently evaluate your past, present, and prepare for the future. As a mom, unfortunately, you do not have the leisurely of putting off tomorrow, as others, what is needed for today.

As a mom, you must understand that the world overwhelms you daily, not necessarily by choice but definitely by force. As a mom, you realize that there are only 24 hours in a day but your efforts from your love and care for another, exudes 48 hours of efforts in a 24-hour period.

As a mom because you want to do so much for so many in the few hours of the day, you Mom, as a person get lost and have a hard time finding balance. As a mom, in a 24-hour period, you may on average you an hour to yourself which is either because of a lunch break or the drive to and from home and even with that, most mom's minds are racing at 1000 miles a minute.

As a mom, you must find time for yourself to balance harmony in your life and to revitalize your mind, body, soul, and spirits. Here are a few tips to balance your life as a mom:

1. WHO Am I - meaning identify what in life makes you happy (i.e. working out, sports, writing, drawing, alone time, meditation), etc.

2. Think Critically - Review your schedule, examine the best time of the day that provides you a time to enjoy the thing you identified in the Who Am I section. That time maybe in the early morning, late at night, or dead smack in the middle of the day.

3. Team Building - Now that you have a plan in place, you must know reach across the party lines to include people that can help you out, whether it is with your schedule or simply assisting you with time for yourself.

4. Cultural Diversity - Through this exploration stage, understand the dynamics of the diversity within your cultures that will have a positive or negative impact on your overall goal such as who you surround yourself with, the environment you leave your kids in that is different or similar to yours, etc. Doing so can either add to or extract from the lack of balance in one's life.

5. Real Life Events/Spiritual Guidance - As a mom, what happens in the world scares us dearly as we are in the business of protecting our children and our loved ones. Even as Moms, we need an outlet, other than that other human insight and interaction for balance and revitalization; therefore, seek guidance from whatever power higher than self you believe in.

6. Communication - As a mom, mastering the art of communication is a daily struggle especially when it comes to our kids and their success. As a result, learning to how to interact and build relationships and rapport is extremely important. It also provides a sense of peace when the end outcome is a Win-Win for all.

7. Leadership Traits: As a mom, you must know how to lead others around for success. For that to happen, you must examine what your leadership traits and one way is through reflection and journaling.

8. Being Transformational: As a Mom, when you are able to constantly examine yourself, how to make it fit in your life, identify your source of assistance, get to understand the various environments and cues around you, allow the events of the world to guide you but spirit to teach you and keep you humble/grounded, know what leadership traits your possess and how to lead others around you for success through communication, then you are able to be transformational in your own life.

9. Who AM I - 360 Degrees of Evolution: As a mom, the prize in balancing one's life is not the outcome, but the process endured along the way that allows for personal growth and development of the mind, body, soul, and spirit. The person who starts the journey of balancing from the beginning and advances through each stage of this transformational leadership model should not be the same; therefore, allowing the person to go from ordinary person to an extraordinary leader from start to finish.

BECOME A LEADER IN YOUR COMMUNITY

To become a leader in your community, you must be mindful of what you stand for, what you believe in, what difference you want to make, and whom you allow in your circle. However, before any of that happens, you must first explore the quality of your inner being. Being a leader in your community requires balancing your personal, social, and professional areas. While each of these components differs in execution, they are all very well connected to YOU.

Being a leader requires finesse, balance, and support. It requires that you understand the question, WHO AM I? Only you can answer that question, and how often you evaluate the question is a critical component of your success. Being a leader in the community requires a strong foundation of time management, organization, and communication skills. Leading in the community requires understanding, knowing, and valuing diversity from others and self; being familiar with your leadership traits while valuing and practicing team building. Above us, be transformational in your position versus transactional. If you cannot say unequivocally, I can do all these things (traits, etc.), then keep on working on it to become a leader in your community.

The problem for those who cannot answer the above with a resounding yes to most if not all things is that people often take on positions and roles to believe the position/role held will make them a leader. This could be far from the truth. To be a leader and an effective one, you must already possess certain traits and characteristics that will add value to the position.

To be a leader in your community, you must clearly understand the diversity in your surroundings. Diversity in education levels, socioeconomic status, cultural backgrounds and environments, communication barriers, and belief systems. As a leader in your community, you can be at the table with people of vast backgrounds, ethnicities, cultures, genders, etc., who support the exact cause but are filled with their prejudices and biases. Your job as the leader in your group is to transform the environment and bring everyone on one accord, despite their differences and similarities. It would be best if you were transformational in your efforts versus transactional. You, as the leader, cannot appear biased, prejudiced, show favoritism or one-sided, or you will lose support and respect quickly.

To be a leader in your community, you should build on your success through volunteer positions early on in your career. The most outstanding leaders were all once loyal and faithful followers. Even the most well-known and respected leaders today remain in the position of a student and teacher. Before becoming a leader or while you are leading a charge in your community, continue to volunteer your efforts in areas where you will continue to be in a position to grow and prosper.

To be a leader in your position, under the many languages spoken by others such as politics, inner-city, foreign language, cultural language, environment language, social cues, to name a few. There are cultures inside of cultures hidden by more cultures in the world, and your job is to become aware, acquainted, and married to these cultures to be successful as a leader in your community. Two of the greatest gifts you can possess as a leader in your community are being well-versed in cultural diversity and communication.

To be a leader in your community, you must be willing and open to being stretched outside your normal comfort zone. To be a leader in your community, you must learn not to use people for selfish gain and to be selfless in your actions. To be a leader in your community, you must remain optimistic and pessimistic in nature and execution. To be a leader in your community, you must critically think through tough decisions and understand tough decisions are not always favorable to followers.

BECOME A BETTER STUDENT

To become a better student, you must quickly realize what your interests are and are not. You must understand which subjects most hold your interest versus those that do not. You must understand that even those subjects you do not have the most significant interest in have a greater interest in you. What does that mean, you wonder? It simply means that all subjects are vital to your existence, success as a student, and becoming a productive member of society.

WHO AM I?

Subjects such as reading, math, science, social studies, physical education, home economics, business, and woodshop, to name a few, all teach you ways to think, act, and problem solve through situations. You use each of the subjects previously mentioned in life daily in different ways and with different people. School provides universal principles of one's life that will only expand beyond graduation, but the foundation is set while in school.

CRITICAL THINKING

To become a better student, you must learn to follow the policy and procedures of life.
You must understand that even policies and procedures you do not believe in or those you find irrelevant are relevant to your life. Much like the discussion above, policies and procedures are in place to protect you and ensure you become successful in life.

REAL-LIFE EVENTS

Policies and procedures were put in place by your forefathers as a guide for success because they had already experienced the trial and tribulations of downfalls and uprises, setbacks and comebacks, peaks and valleys, and want you to be successful. The policies and procedures set in place ensure you go from where you are and reach where you are destined to go on a path of less resistance. Life, as you know it as a student, is desired because others are responsible for you until you turn the appropriate age to care for yourself.

Once you reach that age of maturity, the policies and procedures of life require that you adhere to them appropriately or face the consequences of reality.

To be a better student, adhere to the teachings of your parents and adults around you. To be a better student, you must be an all-around better person. A student is merely a hat you wear and a role in life you play, but underneath that role, "YOU," the person remains. There are people placed in your life to guide you, protect you, and facilitate your path, but you do not have to listen to them, and often, students do not listen to the adults in their lives without hesitation or resistance.

TEAM BUILDING

To be a better student, do not fear help from others or asking for help for success. To be a better student, you must learn to communicate with others around you when help is needed. There will be times left when you are unsure of a problem in a subject, in life, in a situation, with people, and knowledge from another is required. It does not make you less of a person to ask for assistance. It does not make you weak, and it does not make you less of a man or less of a woman; it simply means you are smart enough to know you cannot do things alone.

COMMUNICATION

Communication, like money, can be the root of all evil and success. Communication, unlike money, is the root of all evil and success. In life, there is no "I" in the team, and as the person leading the charge, you must know how to chat with people. You must learn to talk "to people" and not "at people!" You must learn to communicate with people who wear suits, people who wear jeans and a t-shirt, people who hold positions higher than yours, or you hold a position higher than them. When the dust settles and the smoke clears, the language spoken should be universal, making you part of the norm and not the exception, and that is the universal language of "RESPECT!"

If you do not learn how to communicate effectively with others, your career, and the impact of your success as a student can be over even before it starts. The best measure is how you communicate with others if first you learn to communicate with your parents at home.

EXCEL IN THE WORKPLACE

To excel in the workplace, you must be able to answer the inquiry, WHO AM I? Are you a lazy person? Are you a person who likes to be or needs to be micromanaged? Are you an independent or dependent thinker? Are you one that shows up on time, misses time from work, expects a raise but does have the required work? Are you true to yourself and your values? Are you know what skill set you have to offer or further need to develop? What do you know about yourself, and are you honest about it?

If you are unsure who you are and what you have to offer, you must critically think about how to improve upon your foundation for success. For example, if you are often late to work and expect to be there on time, you must first learn to adhere to policy and procedures that govern the workplace to advance. If you demonstrate you are a misfit (someone that cannot fit the norm like others) that cannot follow the basic requirements for success, then excelling in the workplace may not happen as quickly as one would like or even at all.

To excel in the workplace but remain unsure of who you are, you must seek assistance from others for help. You must be willing to release ego and pride to build a support team for your success. While Rome was not built overnight, feedback from a team of peers for success can. This would require you to step outside of your comfort zone and align yourself with those who can provide quality feedback that is honest and constructive; however, you must be ready for the feedback, good, back, or indifferent. Peers are always helpful in providing best practices to others, and it is just a matter of them being asked the question.

To excel in the workplace, you must understand the cultural diversity in your environment. Once you have identified the cultural barriers, you must position yourself to either one side (left vs. right) or remain neutral. Every organizational cultural setting has "cliques," These cliques form their own identity that can help or harm one's career, reputation, and status. Cliques are people who appear to have something in common and stick together as they share the same issues, etc. Positioning yourself for a winning outcome is essential, and all it takes is that you get to know the environment in which you work. The great thing is that it will not take long to figure it out, or it will figure you out.

To excel in the workplace, you must know the leadership qualities you possess and those you quickly acquire to succeed. Every person has a specific skill set and ability that sets them apart. It is not only enough to know your skill sets, but you must understand how to use them to make you an asset to your organization and, ultimately, yourself.

To excel in the workplace, you must know how to communicate on all levels, to varying audiences, in a professional and non-threatening manner. To excel in the workplace, you should not speak to your boss as you would your co-worker because their positions and roles are different. To excel in the workplace, an email you send to someone you are dating that is a co-worker should be vastly different than sending one to a co-worker that you are not dating. To excel in the workplace, the tone used by a person whose job is in the IT department will be different from a person whose responsibility is customer relations. To excel in the workplace, you must know how to be respectful when communicating versus disrespectful regardless of your targeted audience.

To excel in the workplace, you must be transformational in your efforts. There are two sides to this concept (1) as it relates to self and (2) as it relates to the organization. Being transformational in an environment or setting is simply exerting the POWER you possess outwardly for others to gravitate towards acceptance and embrace. Your passion, purpose, finesse, positive energy, and even charisma are what people gravitate to in life and especially in the workplace. No one wants to work with someone that is a 24/7 Grumpster.

The POWER you possess, when exerted, resonates in behavior, interactions, decision making, and even communications and transforms others around you through connections made. Being transformational within the organization requires that you act more on behalf of those you are responsible for as a leader than yourself. In other words, don't be selfish but selfless. Make decisions that will benefit the cause versus any one individual. Being transformational in an organization, especially in a leadership position, can be challenging. Still, it does not have to be if you remain true to yourself and are not swayed by politics.

To excel in the workplace, one must view the environment as one where real-world events occur daily. What happens at work is happening worldwide and should be handled with care. Many people in life, not all, view their workplace as they do their lives. Not many can separate and do separate the two, but they should. When this happens, people view their workplace as their lives, their behaviors, values, actions, and decision-making begin to overlap, and the potential for conflict arises. What can you learn from people in your workplace to excel further? First and foremost, you can learn to be true to yourself and act, behave, and treat others accordingly as you would want to be treated.

"The reason that minorities and women don't have a better shot at getting elected to the Senate or to statewide office is because the campaign finance rules are so skewed as to make it very difficult for non-traditional candidates to raise the money necessary to get elected."

-Carol Moseley Braun

FROM ORDINARY TO EXTRAORDINARY

Someone asked the author, "360 degrees of evolution -wouldn't that put you on the same spot?" The author's answer was, "ABSOLUTELY.... YES, what happens is that the person exits as a new creature after going through the evolutionary process that warrants the change in between" they end right back on the same spot but with a different outlook of self. Now let us dive deeper into the nine core pillars chosen for these transformational leadership models and further understand why they are so significant in developing you as a leader.

Each module is an independent pillar of its own but depends on one another for success as a leader. The core pillars of my DTD's Transformational Leadership Models have been discussed in this book individually. Through stories and real-life scenarios, the model has been shared in practical application in how they work together to have ordinary people transformed into extraordinary leaders by experiencing the 360 Degrees of Evolution.

The DTD's Transformational Leadership Models are universal across industries and disciplines and apply to individuals from individuals such as youth to CEOs of corporations.

This book should be used interchangeably in academic settings and business cultures and environments. The contents of this book can be used as part of the curriculum for youth in primary grades and on secondary levels for those individuals going through workforce development programs, students pursuing advanced degrees, for individuals looking to start a business, enhance their business, or climb that ladder of success in positions within their corporate settings.

The DTD's Transformational Leadership Models' core pillars focus on the personal growth and development of a person and their behaviors. The book's content can be used as part of any structural program, training, or activity that focuses on improvement of self, soft skills development, and as such, but not limited to professional development, leadership training, personal growth, and development.

Dr. Tekemia Dorsey's (DTD) Transformational Leadership Models are designed to take ordinary people and transform them into extraordinary leaders through 360 degrees of evolution, focusing on nine core pillars.

Let's recap the component of each pillar: Conceptual Component Summaries

1. ***Who Am I?***—The key to being an effective leader is to have a true understanding of who you are as an individual and the roles that you play in your life circles. Participants begin to make the connections between their individual identities and the roles they play in their lives.

2. ***Critical Thinking***—In order to develop a true understanding and application of the key components and characteristics of transformational leadership, participants explore the ways that they process and learn information in a variety of situations to develop a fundamental understanding of the ways in which they process information to make decisions as transformational leaders.

Through an examination of Gardner's theory of Multiple Intelligences and Johari's Windows, participants have the opportunity to create their own strategic learning plan as the precursor to developing strategic plans for groups/teams that they may be leading through their roles as transformational leaders.

3. ***Team Building***—A hallmark of transformational leaders is their ability to bring together individuals within a group to work together, collaborate effectively and ultimately grow into Dr. Tekemia Dorsey's (DTD) Transformational Leadership Models becoming leaders themselves—taking direct responsibility for the outcomes of their actions. Participants examine the dynamics of group interaction and the importance of team building in the transformational leadership process.

4. ***Cultural Diversity***—A good transformational leader must consider the backgrounds and cultural footprints of their team in order to make sound decisions. As part of the unit, participants explore the effect that cultural norms, beliefs, and ways of thinking affect group dynamics and impact leadership decisions across a variety of situations.

5. ***Real World Events***—Participants examine real world events and critically assess the role of leaders in each situation. This examination of real-world application of leadership theory allows participants to further develop their understanding of the concepts presented.

6. ***Leadership Attributes***—Participants examine the actions of leaders and have an opportunity to speak to community leaders to further develop their concept of the characteristics and roles of transformational

leaders.

7. ***Communication***—Participants examine the various ways in which messages are communicated—both verbal and nonverbal and assesses their ability to communicate and interact effectively with various groups. The importance and role of communication in leadership is explored, and participants have the opportunity to develop their own theories and strategies to improve communication within a group.

8. ***Being Transformational***—This component provides participants with a way of putting the theory of Johari's Windows into practice and identify various ways in which they can be transformational leaders in their communities.

9. ***Who Am I***—This component provides participants with an opportunity to express who they are as transformational leaders, after have gone through each of the core pillars through this transformational leadership model.

You can surmise from the conceptual summaries of the core pillars; numbers 1 & 9 are both the same and that is not by mistake but rather by divine intervention.

Individuals begin the process of transformational leadership but exits the process as a new creature of habit and having experience 360 Degrees of Evolution. The 360-Degrees of Evolution occurs, when and only when, the individual is honest with self by identifying his/her strengths, areas of weaknesses and remains optimistic to change from stage one of the leadership model.

The nine core pillars of these transformational leadership models are not meant to be a means to an end, but a steppingstone or a continuation of self-exploration with a focus of leadership that leads to positive change and outcomes in one's life. Any of the core pillars can be made interchangeable with other pillars, models, or programs to add a stronger value to the objective and goal at hand.

References

Bauwens, J. and Hourcade, J. (1992). School-based sources of stress among elementary and secondary at-risk students. The School Counselor, 40. 97-102.

Bryson, C. & Hand, L. (2007). The role of engagement in inspiring teaching and learning. *Innovations in Education and Teaching International, 44*, 349-362.

Cochran, J. L. (1996). Using play and art therapy to help culturally diverse students overcome barriers to school success. The School Counselor, 43. 287-297.

Dorsey, T. (1997). The roles and functions that school counselors play in preventing and remediating stressors among middle school students. Fulfillment for Master of Education Degree in Guidance and Counseling, Education Department at the University of Maryland Eastern Shore. Princess Anne, MD 21853

Dorsey, T. (2006). The academic achievement differences of racial/ethnic and gender of 5th grade students: A phenomenological case study. Fulfillment for Doctorate of Management in Organizational Leadership Degree at The University of Phoenix.

Dorsey, T. (2015). From ordinary to extraordinary using Dr. Tekemia Dorsey's (DTD) transformational leadership models 360 degrees of evolution. The Creative GRP, LLC Publishing Company.

Durkheim, E. (1933). Émile Durkheim on The division of labor in society. New York, Macmillan.

Elkind, D. (1986). Stress and the middle grader. The School Counselor, 33. 196 – 206.

Karnes, F. and Bean, S. (1997). Methods and Materials for Teaching the Gifted. Prufrock Press, Inc.

Kinselica, M. S., Stanley, B. B., Thomas, R. R., and Reedy, S. (1994). Effects of Stress moculation training on anxiety, stress, and academic performance among adolescence. Journal of Counseling Psychology, 41(2). 334 - 342

Kopala, M., Esquivel, G., and Baptiste, L. (1994). Counseling approaches for immigrant children. Facilitating the acculturation process. The School

Counselor, 41. 352 – 359.

Gambone, M. A., Klem, A. M., & Connell, J. P. (2002). Finding Out What Matters for Youth: Testing Key Links in a Community Action Framework for Youth Development, Philadelphia: Youth Development Strategies, Inc., and Institute for Research and Reform in Education, Philadelphia, PA.

Halsted, J. (1990). The ERIC Clearinghouse on disabilities and gifted education (**ERIC**). EC Digest #E481

Henderson, P. A., Kelbey, T. J. and Engrebretson, K. M. (1992). Effects of a stress control program on children/s locus of control, self-concept, and coping behavior. The School Counselor, 40. 125 -130

Lupton-Smith, H. S., Carruthers, W. L., Flythe, R., Goetee, E., and Modest, K. H. (1996). Conflict resolution as peer mediation. Programs for elementary, middle, and high school students. The School Counselor, 43. 374 – 389.

Omizo, M. M., and Omizo, S. A., Suzuki, L. A. (1988). Children and stress: An exploratory study of stressors and symptoms. The School Counselor, 35. 267 – 274.

Simons, H., Simons, B. J. and Dorsey, T. (2020). Thought Leader. The Creative GRP, LLC Publishing Company.

Sipe, C., MA, P., and Gambone, M. (1998). Support for youth: A profile of three communities. Public/Private Ventures, Philadelphia, PA.

Tinto, V. (2009, February). Taking student retention seriously: Rethinking the first year of university. Paper presented at the FYE Curriculum Design Symposium 2009, Queensland University of Technology, Brisbane, Australia. Retrieved March 4, 2009, from http://www.fyecd2009.qut.edu.au/resources/SPE_VincentTinto_5Feb09.pdf

USDHHS (U. S. Department of Health and Human Services) (1996). Physical Activity and Health: A Report of the Surgeon General. Washington DC: USDHHS.

Wehmeyer, M. L., Agran, M. and Hughes, C. (1998). Teaching self-determination to students with disabilities: Basic skills for successful transition. Paul H. Brookes Publishing Co

Dr. Tekemia Dorsey's (DTD) Transformational Leadership Models
360 Degrees of Evolution

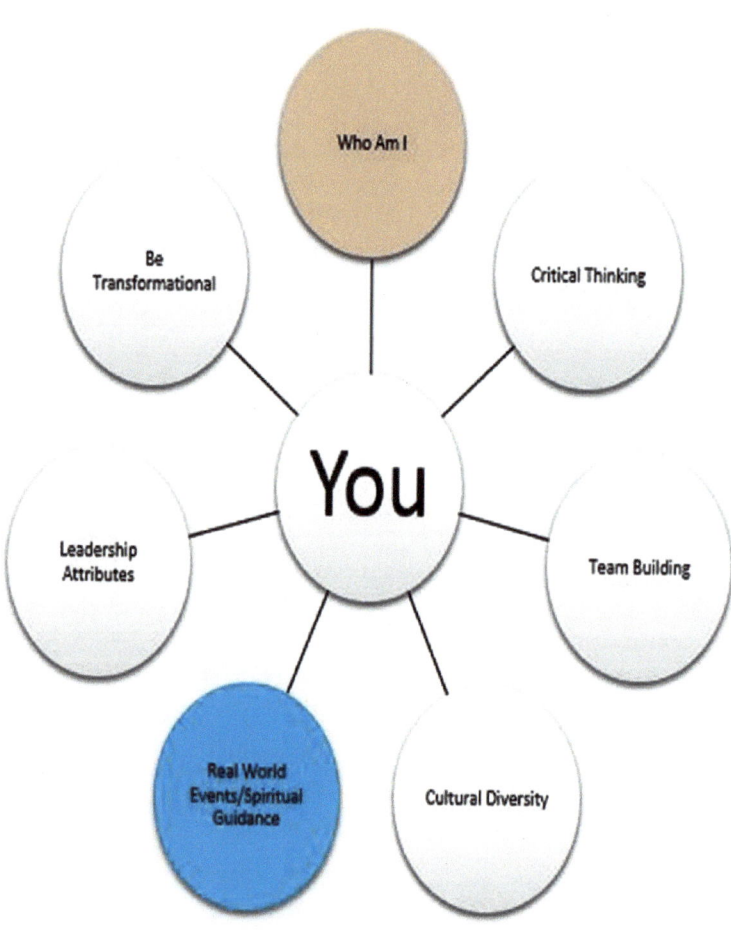

Check out other books in our series.
www.urbanmultisportconsulting.com

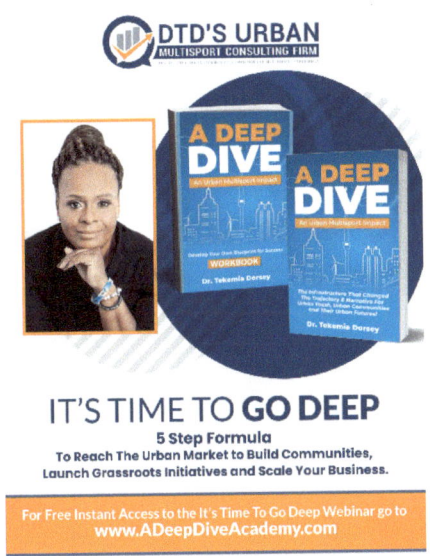

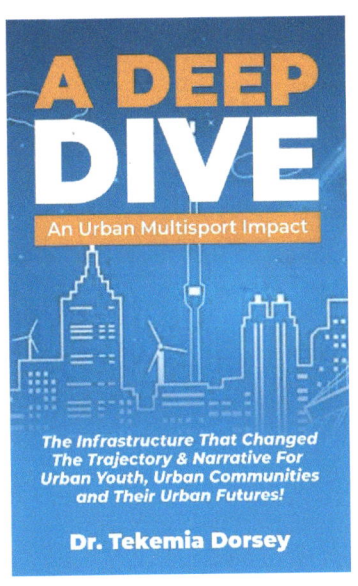

www.ingramcontent.com/pod-product-compliance
Lightning Source LLC
Chambersburg PA
CBHW041352290426
44108CB00006B/129